THE OTHER CALIFORNIA

D0462006

Western Literature Series

Other Books by Gerald W. Haslam

FICTION
Okies: Selected Stories
Masks: A Novel
The Wages of Sin: Collected Stories
Hawk Flights: Visions of the West
Snapshots: Glimpses of the Other California
The Man Who Cultivated Fire and Other Stories
That Constant Coyote: California Stories
Many Californias: Literature from the Golden State (ed.)

NONFICTION
Forgotten Pages of American Literature (ed.)
The Language of the Oil Fields
Western Writing (ed.)
California Heartland: Writing from the Great Central Valley
  (co-ed.)
Literary History of the American West (co-ed.)
*Voices of a Place: Social and Literary Essays from the Other
  California*
Coming of Age in California: Personal Essays
The Great Central Valley: California's Heartland

The Other California

THE GREAT CENTRAL VALLEY IN LIFE AND LETTERS

Gerald W. Haslam

UNIVERSITY OF NEVADA PRESS
RENO   LAS VEGAS   LONDON

WESTERN LITERATURE SERIES EDITOR: JOHN H. IRSFELD

A list of titles in the series appears in the back of the book.

The Other California: The Great Central Valley in Life and Letters by Gerald W. Haslam was originally published in 1990 by Joshua Odell Editions, Capra Press, of Santa Barbara, California. The 1994 University of Nevada Press enlarged edition incorporates six new essays and minor editorial changes throughout the text; new front matter and a newly designed dust jacket reflect the new publisher.

The paper used in this book meets the requirements of American National Standard for Information Sciences—Permanence of Paper for Printed Library Materials, ANSI z39.48-1984. Binding materials were selected for strength and durability.

LIBRARY OF CONGRESS CATALOGING IN PUBLICATION DATA
Haslam, Gerald W.
   The other California: the great central valley in life and letters
/ Gerald W. Haslam.
       p.   cm.
   Originally published: Santa Barbara, California: Capra Press 1990
   ISBN 0-88496-321-7
   1. San Joaquin River Valley (Calif.)—Description and travel.
   2. San Joaquin River Valley (Calif.)—Social life and customs.
   3. San Joaquin River Valley (Calif.)—Literary collections.
F868.S173H37   1990
979.4'8—dc20   CIP

University of Nevada Press, Reno, Nevada 89557 USA
Copyright © 1990, 1994 Gerald W. Haslam
Copyright © 1994 James D. Houston
Copyright © 1978 Jerry McMillan
All rights reserved
Cover art: *California* (1978) Jerry McMillan. Photograhic print. Sulfide duotone from a black and white photographic print, 20″ × 16″. Collection of the Oakland Museum, Prints and Photographs Fund.
Cover design by Susan Gutnick
Printed in the United States of America
9 8 7 6 5 4 3 2 1

For W. H. Hutchinson, "Hutch" . . .
This Valley isn't the same without him.

Contents

Foreword

Gerald W. Haslam is one of those passionately territorial writers the American West is noted for. His territory happens to be the onetime inland sea that stretches from Mount Shasta in the north to Fort Tejon in the south. Writers have been looking at this part of the world for over two hundred years, but I know of no other single writer who has explored it so consistently and with such a knowledgeable eye for its many coexisting layers. In both fiction and nonfiction, as essayist and storyteller, as reviewer and editor, as traveler and interviewer, as lifetime observer and unrepentant native son, Haslam has laid a powerful claim on this long and fertile realm he calls "The Other California."

I met his stories first. This was early in 1975. I was teaching a fiction-writing course at the University of California, Santa Cruz. One spring afternoon a student—a California native by the way, a voracious reader who took great pride in finding the juicy title you had not heard of yet—came into my office with a knowing grin and said, "Here's one you're really going to like," and handed me a copy of *Okies*.

I did not know Haslam's writing, but I knew something about Okies. My dad was born in Durant, Oklahoma, and spent much of his boyhood working farmland east of Fort Worth, where my granddad sharecropped cotton. He had come west in the early 1930s, along with my Alabama mother and a couple of west Texas uncles. I dived into these short stories with a mixture of delight and the kind of involvement that comes from the deep recognition of a way of seeing. Only by chance had I been born in San Francisco instead of Oildale or Bakersfield or somewhere farther north along U.S. Highway 99. Though I did not grow up in the Central Valley, as Haslam did, I knew his people, I knew their music. I knew these fathers and mothers and truckers and working stiffs, and their voices and the things they could not voice.

As soon as I finished the final story I shot off a letter to the publisher and asked, "Who is this guy? What else does he do, and where can I find him?" A while later the publisher wrote back with a Petaluma phone number (just two area codes away), and a note saying something to the effect that the author of *Okies* was an easygoing fellow who would surely enjoy hearing my reactions to his work—a fellow, moreover, who was not opposed to the occasional long-neck bottle of Lone Star or Bud and who could also be counted on for some rather strong opinions about country-western singing, past and present.

A week or so later I called him, and we talked for quite a while. He had recently edited a collection of essays called *Western Writing* for the University of New Mexico Press. A long piece about the little-known town of Taft would also soon be coming out in *The Nation* (included in this volume as "Oil Town Rumble"). And his next project was going to be a collection of prose and poetry from the San Joaquin Valley. There wouldn't be much money in it, but this wasn't going to hold him back. I could tell by the way he talked that it was a labor of love. He foresaw a multiethnic anthology that would open some people's eyes. "A lot of great writing has come from there," he said, "but nobody knows about it yet. Or at least they don't see the Valley as a literary region. But it is, and it's about time somebody got the word out."

We began to talk about literary regions, about how so much

of American literature has had a strong regional base, and about the dialogue that is always going on between writers and certain places. The region can shape a writer, we agreed, and the writer in turn can give a kind of voice to the region and affect the way we see it and think about it.

As we talked, I quickly realized two things. One, here was a Central Valley aficionado, a nut for his home territory, who was going to edit this collection not because anybody asked him to do it, but because he had to. Two, and here was a man after my own heart, when he talked about these things there was excitement in his voice. Another listener might not have described it that way, but I heard it instantly, a subdued and understated southwestern kind of excitement I'd heard in my father's voice at certain times, such as the day he first mentioned a trip we might be making back to Texarkana to meet with relatives he hadn't seen in fifteen years.

I also heard the pioneer's excitement of having come upon some uncharted terrain. Bear in mind that this was 1975. Not many people were talking about regions then, literary or otherwise, at least not in loud voices. "Sense of place" was still a term you used cautiously, and among allies you felt you could trust. Why? Because words like *place* and *region* were always in danger of being equated with *local color* and *provincial*. The anthology that was soon to become *California Heartland* (Capra Press, 1978) was still a dream, gathering momentum in Gerry Haslam's filing cabinet. But this dream was right in sync with a widespread re-recognition and reclaiming of the many regions and subregions of America that was just about to find a wider voice.

It is related, in my own memory, to the photos that the NASA satellite gave us back in 1967, the first photos of Earth as seen from outer space, showing us how finite this globe appears when seen from somewhere else. These photos awakened something. As they moved into wider circulation they began to change forever our ways of looking at the home planet and triggered a gradual rediscovery of the Earth, the whole of it, as well as the various local chunks we inhabit and become intimate with. The emblematic statement from that era was *The Whole Earth Catalog,* which came out in 1968 and won a National Book Award. It is more than coincidence that not long afterward a magazine appeared in Palo Alto called *Place.* I still have some back issues here, a small-press publication featuring earthy and down-home content, in large format, with a high-gloss photo of a bearded farmhand on the cover. The first time I saw that title, with that one word writ large, it went through me like a beam of hot light, illuminating something I had recently begun to sense about my habitat, and which I believe a lot of people were just then starting to sense and to express.

In the past couple of decades, as threats to the physical world have escalated, global consciousness has been on the rise, and so has regional consciousness. No matter where you live these days, some feature of the nearby landscape is under seige— the river, the forest, the meadowland, the seashore, something. This in itself forces us to get better informed, pay closer attention, look at what's right around us before it is changed too drastically, or perhaps disappears forever. The knowledge that we can lose our places has quickened the sense of place and heightened the levels of awareness. This is the main difference between *regionalism* nowadays and the older *provincialism.* Much more is involved than some stubborn attachment to the way your father or your grandfather did things.

And therein lies the value of Gerry Haslam's impressive contribution. He has been true to his obsession with the valley of his birth, a world he knows from top to bottom and from the inside out. Anyone who reads very far into his work must move with him toward a broader sense for what region means. He knows the Central Valley of California from the subsoil up. He knows its range of crops. He knows the waterways and the politics of water, and the politics of runaway growth. He must be the only man alive who is equally conversant with the Fresno poets and the oilfield roughnecks of Kern County. He also knows the ethnic realities, the stories and fates of the indigenous tribes, as well as the fates of the long-gone lakes that, during his childhood, would still fill great patches of the lower San Joaquin. As his work has accumulated, from the mid-1960s onward, he has become a regional writer in the fullest sense of that word. He grasps the myriad details that comprise the surface. He can also dig through the surface of things to tap into the profound matter of how a place shapes lives, characters, actions, dreams, one's sense of history, one's sense of self.

In the collection of essays assembled here, which bring together a lifetime of listening and looking and reading and roaming, we are taken on a journey both outward and inward. Think of it as the account by a traveler who is compelled to describe a long trip he has been on. It is about all that he has seen, the cities and the rivers and the markets and the ghosts. At the same time it is about the effect of these things upon the traveler. In revealing for the rest of us the pulse of California's heartland, he cannot help but reveal his own heart too.

James D. Houston

The Other California

GLIMPSED from an airplane during summer, California's Great Central Valley is a grid of sharply defined, multicolored fields sliding below. Strange machines may crawl over those tracts, dust may billow. But there is dissonance: those geometric parcels are randomly penetrated by disorderly streams, and the impress of old landscapes remains; here, amidst the orderly, imposed patterns of farmland, those natural forms appear as uncontrolled and threatening as malignancies.

Despite the dominance of agriculture, an unresolved conflict with nature limns human illusion in the vast trough, for this place is no more fully tamed than is our own deepest being. To those of us born and blooded in the Valley, those who rough-necked on its oil rigs, who chopped cotton in its fields, who awakened sexually in its riverine forests, this is the heartland of the Golden State, the terrain of our own hearts . . . another, *the* other California.

From above on a winter day a massive gray protozoan appears to have established residence in California's core. What local residents call "tule fog" or "valley fog" has risen from the region's damp, fecund soil, and the earth's surface is engulfed by a ground cloud, producing low-contrast scenes in eerie black and white. William Everson, a distinguished poet born and raised in the Valley, renders it this way: "earth and sky one mingle of color, / See how this moment yields sameness: December evening grayed and oppressive."

Cold seems to invade any clothing during that season and "You can't see but a few feet sometimes," says Earl Wood of Suisun City. At its worst, the miasma closes highways and schools. Relief may come only when rain falls or wind blows. Stockton resident Kathleen Goldman complains, "Fog is depressing. The light of day doesn't change from morning to evening. I can't take it for long."

But winter is by no means the dominant season in this vale. As author Richard Rodriguez, a Sacramento native, recalls, "In almost all my memories, it is warm, it is sunny, it is cloudless." This is for all practical purposes a winter-summer microenvironment, so between a brief, glorious spring, and a short, desiccated fall, sun prevails—some 300 days annually. Rain is rare and heat can be brutal, can bend light rays above neatly furrowed green fields; mirages are everywhere as the earth itself seems to sweat. In the distance, wispy dust devils dance over open tracts. Everything gasps under a faded sky that presses soil, presses leaves, presses breath: heat, heat . . .

Native daughter Joan Didion has written that the Great Central Valley is "so hot that the air shimmers and the grass bleaches white and the blinds stay drawn all day, so hot that August comes on not like a month but like an affliction." That seething, which demands swamp coolers and air conditioners and which, according to Mark Twain, led deceased local residents to send from Hell for their blankets, also stimulates remarkable agricultural verdancy.

The Great Central Valley—a plain some 430 miles long and up to 75 miles wide, surrounded by mountains and covering nearly 15 million acres—has become the richest farming region in the history of the world. By 1985 Fresno County yielded $310.6 million in revenues, Kern County produced $231.2 million, while Kings County contributed $187.6 million—*for cotton alone*; grapes added another $292.1 million to Fresno's tally, $194.8 million to Tulare's, and $152.7 million to Kern's. These are only two of nearly three hundred commercial crops grown locally, so the list could be much, much longer, its line of zeros ever less comprehensible. Suffice it to say that the *annual* value of this area's farm production exceeds the *total* value of all the gold mined in the Golden State since 1848. Moreover, it not only boasts greater agricultural riches than most nations, but its southernmost county, Kern, produces more oil than some OPEC countries . . . another, *the* other, California.

Agriculture dominates, and in this Valley it can hardly be referred to as "farming" in any traditional sense. Richard Smoley, managing editor of *California Farmer*, points out that corporate agriculture here has produced abundantly indeed: "Each farmer feeds 82 people. Americans eat better than citizens of

3

any other nation and pay less." Hereabouts it has developed its own terminology: farms are "ranches," farmers are "growers," farming is "agribusiness."

Agribusiness has been distinctly creative in the Valley, developing unique equipment—the Fresno scraper, the Stockton gangplow, the caterpillar tractor, the Randall harrow, etc. —employing great doses of chemicals, absorbing immense quantities of water and humanity, experimenting with unusual crops. Most significantly, it has become truly big business.

Corporations whose officers are more adept at picking stock options than cotton bolls control great tracts, directing ranch managers who in turn direct laborers. How much land do big enterprises control? In Tulare, Kings, and Kern counties, at the Valley's south end, Don Villarejo of the California Institute for Rural Studies in 1982 found 5,766 farms of 80 acres or less, totaling 234,622 acres, but he also located 26 spreads of 5,121 acres or more which totaled 646,735.

More dramatically, in 1981 two-thirds of the acreage irrigated by the State Water Project in the same region was owned by just eight companies: those "farmers" were Chevron USA (37,793 acres), Tejon Ranch (35,897 acres), Getty Oil (35,384 acres), Shell Oil (31,995 acres), Prudential Insurance (25,105 acres), a foreign conglomerate that operates under the name of Blackwell Land Company (24,663 acres), Tenneco Corporation (20,180 acres), and Southern Pacific Railroad (16,528 acres). Most of them also controlled other substantial tracts elsewhere in the Valley.

Despite domination by huge agribusiness—journalist Robert DeRoos aptly describes them as "agricultural baronies"—many family farms continue to exist. Such people develop an intimate relationship with the soil they work. Says rice grower Francis DuBois of Davis, "I know how that mud feels between my toes and I like it." Aldo Sansoni, who farms near Los Baños,

4

elaborates: "I look out my door . . . I know every inch of this dirt. I don't farm through the windshield of a pickup. I've gotten out there and worked that land for hours on end. I've done the hay. I've picked my share of tomatoes and cantaloupes." That both those family farmers control several thousand acres is indicative of the scale of most successful agriculture hereabouts.

Due to the profligacy of agribusiness, the Great Valley—ironically, a region virtually ignored by California's bleached-blond-and-perfect-tan stereotype—is the state's heartland, its economic hub as well as its physical center. "This is what California is," writes geographer John A. Crow, "a long central valley encircled by mountains." Many visitors, including some Californians, consider it only an open landscape to be endured on the drive to Los Angeles or San Francisco, to Yosemite or Sequoia.

In fact, it is a unique realm, "a sub-region of the American West" according to novelist James D. Houston. Biscuits and gravy for breakfast, or *chorizo con huevos para desayuno*, overshadow champagne brunch here; hard work is admired and soft people are tolerated. This domain remains in many ways closer to Lubbock or Stillwater than to Hollywood. Some commentators argue that harsh weather produces a harsh society, but the continuing existence of a large body of poor, hardworking people—the broad gap between haves and have-nots—provides a more reasoned explanation for the area's rough reputation.

Life has always been both tough and promising in this region. During the winter of 1861–62, the heaviest rainfall in recorded history flooded the Valley. William Henry Brewer, a member of the state's first Geological Survey, noted that the entire area had become a vast lake: "*Steamers* ran back over the ranches fourteen miles from the river . . . to the hills," wrote

5

the young scientist. "Thousands of farms are entirely under water—cattle starving and drowning."

The deluge contributed indirectly to the Valley's eventual agricultural profusion, not only because the dominant cattle industry was crippled but also because, under the dictates of the Swamplands Act then in effect, anyone who could dike and drain wet areas would gain title to them. Opportunists such as the fabled Henry Miller were able to bend the act's intent and acquire immense tracts of normally arid land by claiming them during the flood, then waiting for the normal sparse rainfall pattern to do the rest. Ironically, Miller then had to devise irrigation systems for the erstwhile "swamplands" in order to render them productive.

That story resonates with several enduring Central Valley motifs: the need for irrigation systems and other specialized farming methods, chicanery and huge landholdings concentrated in the hands of few owners (Miller and his partner Charles Lux, for example, would eventually acquire 700,000 acres in the Valley), and, in turn, paternalism and social patterns demanding a large, mobile labor force—frequently populated by nonwhites.

In Brewer's day, the northern portion of the Valley, called the Sacramento for the river that bisects it, was more settled and cultivated; today the south, called the San Joaquin for its major river, evinces more intense development. In the 1860s, the Sacramento Valley was characterized by vast riparian or riverine forests, junglelike woodlands that lined rivers and extended sometimes hundreds of yards inland. Brewer described the area this way: "A wide plain borders the river on each side . . . but generally we saw only the river and its banks, which were more or less covered with trees—willows, cottonwoods, oaks and sycamores—with wild grapes trailing from them." The riparian woodlands, among the richest habitats for

6

animals, were also important factors in natural soil conservation and flood control. Now over 90 percent of riverine forests are gone, as is so much else of this area's natural environment—little noticed, little remembered, little mourned in the celebration over what has been accomplished.

The contemporary San Joaquin Valley to the south—the very *notion* of it—illustrates well the extent of physical and conceptual alteration that has occurred here. It is composed of what were once two distinct geomorphic and ecological entities: the San Joaquin Plain and the now-forgotten Tulare Basin. All rivers in the former drained north into San Francisco Bay; the Valley's four southernmost rivers, however, did not drain at all but formed vast, shallow bodies of water in the otherwise arid Tulare Basin. Today, with its rivers dammed, its lakes drained and their beds tilled by farmers, that basin is indistinguishable from the large plain that fronts it and, in terms of popular perception, it has ceased to exist.

Over a hundred miles north of Tulare Basin, the Sacramento and San Joaquin rivers meet and flow toward San Francisco Bay in the Valley's other major subregion, the Delta. Much developed for agriculture, it is located far inland and composed of a thousand miles of braided river channels, marshes, swamps, and diked "islands"—islands which are frequently *lower* than the surrounding watercourses. It is shaped like a ragged triangle draining from its narrowest point, an inversion of the wide-mouthed form most other deltas assume. Tourists motoring through the Delta are occasionally startled by the sight of large, oceangoing vessels apparently plowing through nearby asparagus fields, some fifty miles inland from the sea—the boats actually traveling a diked channel to or from the landlocked port of Stockton.

When Brewer visited the Valley, he traveled through the Delta on a paddle-wheel steamer, then upriver into the Sacra-

7

mento Valley, entering a region that already had been considerably, if subtly, altered. It was once home to one of the nation's heaviest concentrations of Native Americans, over 100,000 Yokuts, Wintun, Maidu, and Miwok, but by the 1860s their population was in dramatic decline. Spaniards had explored the Valley but never settled and controlled it. Nonetheless, their presence had its effects. The replacement of native perennial grasses by introduced annuals, virtually unnoticed at the time, most characterizes the initial Hispanic influence; early explorers used straw as packing material and their domestic animals were walking seed bags, so the change began as soon as the first of them ventured into this vulnerable region.

Large native animals, like native grasses, were quickly displaced or eliminated—by hunting, by competition from domestic animals, and by habitat destruction. The Valley's prairie, which writer Mark Reisner called "an American Serengeti," was grazed by herds of pronghorn antelope and tule elk, and by mule deer; golden beaver swam in its sloughs. They, in turn, were preyed upon by grizzly bears, coyotes, and cougars. In the southern Valley, great condors cleaned carcasses. Now antelope are gone, condors are gone, grizzlies are long gone. Elk and beaver remain in small preserves. Coyotes and mule deer still ply the Valley's edges. One hunter on the west side of the Valley in 1861 told Brewer that he had killed "seven or eight hundred" deer thereabouts, then complained, "They are getting scarce now."

Today most of the Central Valley is green with field crops, orchards, and groves. Irrigation—agribusiness uses 85 percent of the state's fresh water annually—and other technology here have led to greater and more efficient use of land. A stunning 25 percent of all table foods consumed in the United States are grown in this region. As grower Jack Stone of Fresno County puts it, "You're not going to do that with your hand on a shovel."

The negative side of such abundance is that Valley agriculture has developed a chemical dependency as intense and as potentially destructive as a junkie's. By 1978, for example, growers were spending $1 billion annually for pesticides alone, and today they use approximately one-third of all pesticides produced in America.

Where does that lead? Insect damage has been largely controlled, but more than two-thirds of the water wells tested in Fresno County since 1979—some 1,700—evidence pesticide pollution, as do the streams and reservoirs that drain Valley fields. And increasingly, insects are developing resistance to toxic chemicals, a feat that has so far escaped humans. Three Valley towns—Fowler in Fresno County, McFarland in Kern County, and Earlimart in Tulare County—now evidence mysterious cancer clusters. Says Dr. Vincent Leonardo of Fowler, "The farmers were guilty of polluting the groundwater. But they didn't know it. No one knew it. They felt real bad, and it was in their own wells."

Many feel trapped on the chemical treadmill. Norman Crow of Stanislaus County explains: "As farmers, we're probably the greatest environmentalists. We see every part of every tree, every acre of land. I'd love it if I didn't have to use these chemicals." Experts suggest that using them really isn't necessary if farmers can settle for lower yields over a longer period of time —sustainable agriculture. However, changing farmers' minds may be more difficult than altering technology. As Michael Perleman of Chico State University suggests, "They've had decades of experience with chemicals and forgotten other ways to farm." This is, of course, a national problem, but nowhere does it stand in higher relief than here.

Even the prestigious University of California is now turning some of its research attention away from high tech toward the development of less-damaging alternatives. As Tim Wallace, a UC agricultural economist, concedes, "There is an acceptance that we can't have business as usual." For the time being, however, concentrations of chemicals continue both to stimulate and to taint production, to foul water and soil, to poison wildlife and humans alike. In 1985, for example, more than 300 people were sickened by watermelons to which aldicarb had been applied illegally by Valley farmers. And chemicals aren't the only sources of environmental problems in this man-made garden.

Irrigation here has involved uncontrolled pumping from deep, ancient stores of groundwater, leading to soil subsidence; the south Valley's surface has drooped thirty feet in some places because of empty pore space in the drained aquifers. Most water now used locally is imported from elsewhere by the Central Valley Project and the State Water Project. It is symbolic of human ingenuity that the latter has produced not only the state's longest stream (the California Aqueduct, a concrete-lined channel 444 miles in length) but the world's highest reverse waterfall (the A. D. Edmonds Pumping Plant thrusts water 1,926 feet *up* the Tehachapi Mountains).

Water is more than a practical necessity in this domain; it is power, so its control remains a major theme. The great irrigation projects never limited distribution to 160 acres per farmer as was statutorily required until 1982, evidence of the political clout of agribusiness. Thus the projects did not have the promised effect of increasing the number of small farms but, according to Villarejo, "did just the opposite, concentrating more land in the hands of fewer—often corporate—growers."

Although more efficient (and more expensive) methods of

watering, such as sprinkler or drip systems, are now available, wasteful flood irrigation continues to be employed here. Where previously arid lands have been saturated, still other problems have developed. Water leaches toxic metals and salts, which can kill the land's ability to grow crops. "In the rich San Joaquin Valley," points out Lowell Lewis, director of the University of California's Agricultural Experiment Station, "more than 400,000 acres are now seriously affected by salt. It is projected that by the turn of the century . . . another million acres could be lost to salinity."

The traditional solution for such problems has been drains that remove polluted water, ultimately shipping it toward San Francisco Bay, where most of the Valley's rivers drain. On the Valley's southwest side, wastewater flows through the San Luis Drain to Kesterson Reservoir. That runoff has been found to carry toxic concentrations of selenium leached from the soil, and it has killed and maimed water birds, putting the human population on notice that something is seriously amiss.

It is revealing that growers turned to the Bureau of Reclamation and Lawrence Berkeley Laboratory for solutions— "Somehow technology will save us" seems to be an enduring faith in the Valley. Three plans were proposed: a "Wet-flex" option, which would dilute contamination with groundwater; a complicated "Immobilization" plan, which would alter crops, change water levels, and employ chemicals to keep excessive selenium out of the food chain; and a scheme to dry the ponds and scrape their noxious topsoil into a sealed dump.

Then two scientists at the University of California at Riverside, William Frankenberger and Ulrich Karlson, discovered that naturally occurring fungi, which convert the concentrated selenium into a relatively nontoxic gas but do so very slowly, can be speeded up by the addition of more carbon, more oxy-

11

gen, and trace amounts of zinc as a catalyst. Nature itself may provide the best answer, but the present plan is to implement the natural process only after having scraped the dried ponds.

Other, perhaps even more insidious problems, such as air pollution and urban crime patterns, are developing as population increases in this enclosed district. The Valley is filling with people at a rate two and a half times above the state's average. In greater Fresno, for instance, the capital of America's richest farming county, the population is increasing as crops long have, over half a million now, the burgeoning largely based upon agricultural abundance. Along with other rapidly growing cities—Stockton, Bakersfield, Sacramento, Modesto, Chico, Redding—Fresno stands as an avatar because nearly 50,000 acres a year are presently being paved there, much of it productive farmland.

In fact, the Great Central Valley has become California's third great population center. The region is expected to house ten million residents early in the next century, and Arnold "Jefe" Rojas, a ninety-one-year-old vaquero who lived in Wasco, warned, "Someday we will have to plow up the malls to plant something we can eat." Such growth reveals an enduring pattern in this state: rich earth taken out of production, leading to the expensive compensatory development of marginal tracts. For example, when the citrus groves of Orange County in Southern California were uprooted by urban development, orange and lemon groves were planted and fertilized and irrigated on what had previously been considered unpromising Valley land. Now this region is slowly filling with people too.

In 1863, Brewer noted, "The hotel where we stopped showed a truly Californian mixture of races—the landlord a Scotchman, Chinese cooks, Negro waiter, and a Digger Indian stable boy." The population in the Valley remains decidedly multi-ethnic, because this region has attracted the determined and the desperate, willing to toil in its fields, to start at the bottom in an attempt to reap California's rich promise: Chinese, Japanese, Southern European, East Indian, Mexican, Filipino, Okie, Black—more than one hundred distinct groups.

This is not to say that brotherhood reigns supreme; it doesn't, and racist verbiage can even be heard in languages other than English. Nonetheless, opportunities for nonwhites seem to be slowly improving. Today, at packing sheds or fast-food restaurants throughout the Valley, high school kids of dark and fair skin work together, exchange ethnic barbs, even date, and sometimes they fight.

Brewer's 1863 observation reveals one other thing: Already a whites-on-top class system was evolving. While educational opportunity and shared experiences are slowly changing it, the Valley has traditionally boasted a bottom-heavy society built like a pyramid: a tiny elite are its peak; below them, a small middle class providing services; the bulk of the structure and its indispensable foundation, marginal-to-poor people. Each group has been larger and less white than the one above it.

Certainly one aspect of the heat generated when César Chavez's United Farm Workers successfully organized farm labor from a base in Delano was social as well as economic, the status quo threatened by that organization of brown people. Today, the Valley's middle class grows larger and more ethnically diverse, and even the elite is somewhat integrated, although Brewer's "Scotchman" is still far more apt to reside there than is his "Digger Indian."

What has developed in this Valley is a rigorously heterogeneous society that is indeed marred at times by parochialism, xenophobia, and racism, but that is remarkably free from the sweeps and swoops of coastal trendiness. But that may not be true for long, since today, just east of Altamont Pass, the Bay Area is slipping in and the Valley is leaking out, with com-

13

munities such as Tracy, Ripon, Manteca, Patterson, Stockton, Turlock, and Modesto experiencing growth surges fueled in large measure by commuters willing to travel across two ridges of the Coast Ranges to work each day in coastal or bay cities.

Why is this redefinition of region taking place? "The farmers are selling and the developers are buying and the commuters are moving in," explains Brad Bates, mayor of Turlock. By early 1990, 5,000 acres of land in the Stockton area alone was being covered with new subdivisions because, with the average price for houses in the Bay Area swelling to over $200,000, many families were roaming far afield to find affordable domiciles. Sheridan Beuving, a Modesto real estate salesman, explains, "We have a rule of thumb that for every extra mile you drive to the Bay Area, you save $1,000 in the price of a house."

One commuter, Dave Masterson of Ripon, works in faraway Sunnyvale, and he says that beyond lower prices, he likes the quality of life in the Valley: "It's nice to be able to walk down the street and wave at people you know." Not everyone waves, however, since the new, relatively affluent commuters add one more dimension to the existing social and economic tension. Longtime working-class and poor residents alike, many of whom are Hispanic, have seen local housing prices rise dramatically and are, as a result, that much farther from their own hope of owning a home.

Nonetheless, populations in most towns in southern San Joaquin County and northern Stanislaus County continue swelling. In a sense, the communities are already realigning themselves, beginning to leave the agricultural Valley and join the industrialized Bay Area without physically relocating, and that, in turn, challenges previous economic, geographic, and demographic assumptions: What is the Valley? Where is the Bay Area? Asserts Modesto mayor Carol Whiteside: "Whether we like it or not, our region is now far more closely linked to the Bay Area than it is to the rest of the Central Valley." We are seeing California redefine itself here.

Long before freeways allowed commuting, many Valley towns, in a classic western pattern, grew along rail lines or rivers. Bakersfield did both. While agribusinesses such as DiGiorgio Farms, Giumara Brothers, or Tejon Ranch all thrived in part due to the railroad, for local natives the Kern River—called simply and affectionately "the River"—was dominant. "For those of us who live here, to mention the River is to stir up memories," explains Ann Williams, born and raised in Bakersfield. "My father brought home fish and stories from the wildest places on the Kern." For others, it evokes the shared breath of clandestine passion, the devastation of friends drowned, the exhilaration of inner tubes bouncing down rapids. And it evokes enduring sadness, for since it was diverted and dammed, its riparian forest has shrunken to a green memory and little of its water reaches the city once called Kern Island.

Far to the north of erstwhile Kern Island, huge hoary Mount Shasta, a towering deity, seals the Valley's northern end. This mystical mountain, revered by native cultures, dominates the flatland for more than a hundred miles south. Today, air pollution often obscures the massif, and on its shoulder is located the linchpin of the Central Valley Project, Shasta Dam. Gazing back from rising land near the dam, the burnished Sacramento Valley opens on a summer day: A spiral of smoke rises to the west where rice hulls are being burned, a narrow forest serpentines onto the prairie where the mighty river flows, and, below, the Valley's northernmost city, Redding, spreads into the foothills.

At the Valley's other end, writer William Rintoul from Taft looks north from the fabled Cañada de Uvas in the Tehachapi Mountains and observes: "It used to be when I was coming off

15

the Grapevine looking out over the southern San Joaquin Valley on a clear night, I could see only scattered lights. . . . Now there are lights everywhere." Over a hundred and twenty years earlier, Brewer visited the same area and praised the "lovely view of the plain, of Buena Vista Lake, and of the coast ranges."

The plain is still there, though it is now a checkerboard of agricultural variety, and the coast ranges remain, although their slopes are now dotted with oil pumps. Buena Vista Lake, which covered more than 4,000 acres at depths up to ten feet, is gone, its floor now plowed and irrigated and reaped. Few open regions have been more physically altered by technology than this one.

Life in this realm nonetheless remains pleasant and hopeful for most. Summer nights are especially memorable: With darkness concentrating the senses, a drive through fields can be an olfactory adventure—redolent of turned earth, of mowed alfalfa, intimate aromas rich and rank as a lover's breath. They may be sliced momentarily by the sharp stench of imposed chemicals, then through the darkness return those comforting, those titillating scents dense as gravy. Traveling them is a dream journey.

Dawn reveals a vast agricultural panorama—cooled, perhaps, toward the seventy-degree range by gentle darkness. Sleepy irrigators climb from pickups, set water, then rest for a moment against shovels while drinking coffee poured from thermoses or chewing fresh plugs of tobacco. Palpable sweetness lingers in the air then, as the sun sneaks over the ragged Sierra Nevadas to the east, a fragrance of life, of hope, and it is tempting to pretend that larger problems belong elsewhere.

The Lake
That Will Not Die

A BRISK CROSSWIND *tugs at the car as it cruises through rain-cleansed air down Interstate 5 toward Oildale. To the east, the vast San Joaquin Plain is foreshortened all the way to muscular Sierras dusted with snow. Much closer, two long rows of palm trees stand as forlorn sentries along a soggy farm road. We are slipping down the Great Central Valley's western edge along the first rise of treeless western hills, emerald now and dotted with muddy cattle.*

Hurrying south, past multicolored patches of vegetation

flecked with standing water, the rich aroma of wet earth thickens the air; it is a smell, invasive and comforting, that city dwellers do not know. This country boy sucks it hungrily into his lungs.

"What smells so funny?" asks my son, Carlos. "Can I roll the window up?"

"No."

Roadside ditches are full, and occasional mallards and coots can be seen in them, but that does not prepare us for the vision that abruptly appears farther down the freeway: a vast and un-expected sheet of water extending as far as we can see, appearing to fill the entire southern end of the Great Valley.

I nose our car to a stop on the highway's shoulder and Carlos, who has endured this trip many times, asks, "What's all that water, Dad? I don't remember it."

For a moment, I do not answer because we are seeing a ghost. Finally I reply, "Tulare Lake."

▲

Tulare Lake was once the largest body of fresh water west of the Great Lakes. Formed by the entrapped drainage of four Sierra rivers, the Kings, Kaweah, White, and Tule—its highest level was recorded in 1862. That year it covered 486,400 acres to depths exceeding forty feet, actually swallowing two other sig-nificant lakes, 8,300-acre Kern and 4,000-acre Buena Vista, which trapped drainage from the Sierra's longest stream, Kern River, in a sub-basin to the south. In fact, the entire southern end of the Great Valley—120 miles by 50 miles—resembled a primordial sea, its broadened periphery dotted with displaced rabbits and foraging cattle, its shimmering surface darkened by uncountable waterfowl, for this was a linchpin in the Pacific Flyway.

Most wet years well into the late nineteenth century, Tulare

Lake covered 200,000 acres and measured 75 by 25 miles during its high season, ebbing and flowing like a huge tidal pool in the midst of an otherwise desiccated landscape. Historian Frank Latta claims it virtually dried up during prolonged periods of drought. The annual pulsing of local wetlands was determined far less by its scant rainfall than by snowmelt in the southern Sierra Nevada, which fed all the streams that emptied into this basin.

As a result, the region was a land of startling contrasts: vast reed beds, marshes, and ponds surrounded by bleached grassland or land with no grass at all—even sand dunes on the lake's southern and southeastern shores—while mallards and coots and Canadian honkers fed in the proximity of horned toads and jackrabbits. To the east side, along the Kaweah River's alluvial fan, a dense oak forest extended to the water's edge, and alkali flats, like earth crusted with snow, could be found glaring along miles of marshes and sloughs.

Lakes and wetlands were unique features of a remarkable geomorphic amalgam known as Tulare Basin: Tulare Lake Basin to the north, Buena Vista Basin to the south. The northern basin was dominated by the large lake for which it was named. William Preston in *Vanishing Landscapes*, his benchmark study of the locale, describes it this way: "an area delimited on the north, west, and south by the boundaries of Tulare and Kings Counties and on the east by vaguely determined but readily visible limits of cultivation . . . a topographic basin with interior drainage." Buena Vista Basin lay below the present Kern County line, enclosed roughly by the locations of present-day Delano, Wheeler Ridge, Taft, and Buttonwillow. Southeast and southwest of Bakersfield, the aforementioned Kern and Buena Vista lakes collected the flow of Kern River. Between and among those two bodies of water existed many channels, marshes, and swamps, while another good-sized, tule-lined pool called Goose Lake filled to the northwest near Buttonwillow.

During wet years, Buena Vista Slough linked the sub-basins. As geographer Preston explains, despite the distinctness of those sections, "historically the word 'basin' was used to describe the entire southern end of the Valley as a unified landscape." In years of extreme precipitation, such as 1862, the entire territory was a single vast lagoon.

The hub of it all was indeed vast Tulare Lake and its interconnected wetlands: a trough within a basin within a valley. Its volume swelled and shrank and swelled again in the west-center of the basin named for it, extending east from terraces near present-day Kettleman City toward gradually rising terrain adjacent to Corcoran. The site of Lemoore marks the lake's approximate northern boundary, while to the south the state historical monument at Allensworth stands on the edge of what was once shore.

In fact, attendant wetlands extended far south past Buttonwillow in Kern County, east toward Tulare and Visalia, and north along Fish Slough well into Fresno County; the west was sealed by the inner edge of the Coast Range, specifically Kettleman Hills. The Sierra Nevada and the Coast Range are nearly seventy-five miles apart here, deflecting rain clouds from the widened valley, so this is an arid to semiarid realm, a desert, absorbing only five to ten inches of rain annually. Nonetheless, in the past, standing water was its most signal characteristic.

Each spring Tulare Lake would swell with snowmelt, then recede dramatically by fall or early winter. Local pioneers played a kind of agricultural roulette by planting grain as water retreated on the drying lake bed, then harvesting before the next cycle's runoff once more filled the depression—they "plowed pollywogs in spring, and harvested frogs in winter," or so local folklore had it. It was usually a profitable strategy, but not always.

In 1906, for instance, a late date when most of the lake's tributaries had already been diverted for irrigation, William Hubbard found his equipment trapped when water rose faster and higher than expected. Hubbard, who farmed east of Delano and annually planted grain far to the northwest on the lake's rich floor, moved his threshing machines to an island locals had never seen covered with water, then escaped by boat. This was, however, a wet year and soon his gear was six feet below the lake's surface—an appropriate depth since all the machinery was ruined and so was the farmer. Eventually the rusted equipment was dragged back to his yard where it stood for years, known as Hubbard's Junkpile.

The diversion of tributaries for irrigation had begun in the 1870s. That same surface water could no longer flow directly into Tulare Lake, which as a result suffered a steady decline not only in quantity but also in quality, because irrigation runoff leached salts from alkali soil. Streams continued to be diverted into this century, and soon diminished runoff could no longer dilute intensified salinization; at the turn of the century the lake was too saline to support significant aquatic life, and its once-thriving commercial fishery was finished.

Thirty years later, Kings River—the lake's most important source of water—was irrigating more land than any other stream in the world except the Nile and Indus rivers, over a million acres. Little wonder then that only a piddling flow ever reached the old lake bed most years and, as Donald Worster points out, "that destroyed grower unity, and overloaded the courts" because ex-partners battled over limited resources. When dams such as Pine Flat and Isabella were finally built on major streams thirty-plus years ago, they served as the coups de grace in a process of diminution that had begun nearly a century earlier.

Today, reclaimed and plowed and planted, the old lake bed is farmland. Cotton and safflowers are produced where fish were once netted. In fact, the very existence of that vast sheet of water is but a vague memory, which dramatically demonstrates how much humans have altered even this open terrain in California's core. Someone driving through the Central Valley today isn't apt to recognize that only 4 percent of the landscape is estimated to remain unaltered: nearly all of its natural wetlands are gone, nearly all of its native grasslands no longer exist, nearly all of its oak woodlands have been destroyed. In the nineteenth century, hogs were run on Atwell's Island southeast of Tulare, and no fences were needed because the settlement could be reached only by boat; today the island is a dryland farming town called Alpaugh.

▼

"Back in 1955, right after I finished high school," I tell Carlos, who thinks the fifties were neat, *"a couple of buddies and I drove up to Alpaugh to do some duck hunting. I'd heard a pal of my dad's say there were lots of them at a place called Tulare Lake.*

"Well, we crisscrossed dirt roads, drove along miles of ditches and sloughs, saw a million red-winged blackbirds and a billion tules, and one mudhen.

He laughs, "Only one mudhen?"

"More than one. Anyway, we were half-lost and felt like we were in the middle of nowhere, so when we finally ran into an old black man fishing in a canal, I stopped the car and went to talk with him. I started out by asking him if he'd caught any fish, and he smiled and showed me some small catfish he had in a bucket.

"Then I told him we were looking for ducks, and he smiled again: 'They's ducks all over here.'

"That led me to ask him where Tulare Lake was, and he said, 'It ain't here no mo'.' The finality of those words—'no mo''—has stuck with me ever since. We never did see the lake."

Carlos gazes at me, then asks, "And then what happened?" He has seen many movies and expects action.

"Nothing," I admit. "We went home."

▲

Tulare Lake Basin is now indistinguishable from the San Joaquin Plain that borders it to the north. Just above the alluvial fan that separates those two geomorphic regions, the San Joaquin River crosses the dominant prairie, then winds north along the Valley's western edge. Tributaries in that flat realm all drain into San Francisco Bay, and open grassland—not standing water—characterizes it. In 1861, William Henry Brewer described the San Joaquin as "a plain of absolute desolation." Today those two distinct environs—the barren plain and the boggy basin—have been rendered indistinguishable by development and reclamation, and they are lumped under a single name: the San Joaquin Valley.

Yet Tulare Lake Basin, also called Tulare Valley, once boasted its own distinct regional identity. An 1888 *Business Directory and Historical and Descriptive Hand-Book of Tulare County, California,* for instance, advised local residents, "All Tulareans should co-operate in giving the name of their great valley a wide and honorable notoriety, leaving the inhabitants of the San Joaquin to look out for the name and fortune of their portion of the state."

It is more than a little ironic that the same publication would complain about the lake itself, by then already diminished by

23

stream diversion and considered an impediment to agricultural development: "the one natural feature of the county that our conscience will not let us praise. . . . It is a great unsightly mudhole."

Historically, although the huge lake was its nucleus, the basin housed those rich, complicated wetlands that included numerous freshwater aquatic communities. Marshes were defined by warm, shallow water clogged with dense masses of sedges, cattails, rushes, reeds, and other aquatic vegetation— the generalized "tulares" for which the Spanish named this region. Small local swamps added trees and shrubs where riparian forests met marshes. Wildlife abounded in both. There were also many boggy ponds, convoluted sloughs or channels; everything was poorly drained and seasonal.

Floating "islands" of tules, many large enough to support the weight of several people, are reported to have drifted windblown across Tulare Lake's surface. Those bulrushes decomposed in the water, enriching it with their nutrients and triggering a complex and abundant food chain. Little wonder, since tules, some growing to a height of twenty feet, surrounded the water in unimaginable profligacy. In 1850, U.S. Army surveyor George Horatio Derby said he had to fight his way through a dense, two-mile-wide band of tules to reach open water on Tulare Lake. In *The Land of Little Rain* (1903), novelist Mary Austin described that ribbon of vegetation this way:

> *ghostly pale in winter, in summer deep, poisonous-looking green, the waters thick and brown, the reed beds breaking into dingy pools, clumps of rotting willows, narrow winding water lanes and sinking paths. The reeds grow inconceivably thick in places, standing manhigh above water; cattle, no, not any fish nor fowl can penetrate them.*

The region's long summers created a semitropical environment as cold snowmelt water sat among decaying vegetation in poorly drained, shallow beds, where it warmed and evaporated, so diseases such as malaria were a menace. Zephryn Englehardt reports that malaria and cholera epidemics killed nearly three-quarters of the area's abundant Indian population in 1832–33.

Despite such pestilence, there was prescience in William Henry Brewer's observation: "The soil is fertile enough, but destitute of water, save the marshes near the river and near Tulare Lake." The dry land was indeed fertile, as development has proved, but Brewer added a caveat: "The marshy region is unhealthy and infested with mosquitoes in incredible numbers and of unparalleled ferocity. The dry plain on each side abounds in tarantulas."

During most years, the fluctuating water of Tulare Lake was plied by steamboats and various other vessels, since the lake sent waterfowl, fish, frogs' legs, and even turtles to faraway dining establishments. An 1883 history of Kern County proudly states:

> *From Tulare Lake come the turtles that make the rich turtle soups and stews in San Francisco hotels and restaurants. . . . These turtles are sent in sacks to San Francisco. During the Season more than 180 dozen found a ready sale at the bay.*

Local Indians, the Yokuts, had developed buoyant tule rafts with holes in their floors through which they could spear fish. After American settlement and control, professional fishermen during the 1870s and 1880s claimed to have caught up to eight tons of fish from the lake with only one haul of a horse-drawn seine.

In the old days, game was abundant here and the Yokuts had no tales of starvation in their repertoires. They were considered fortunate indeed by tribes dwelling in the surrounding hills. This area was also seen as a paradise by early American trappers and hunters. Beavers and otters were so common in the 1820s, for instance, that Jedediah Smith once took 1,500 pounds of pelts in a single tour. In 1844, John Charles Frémont was astounded by "multitudes of wild fowl, principally geese." Tule elk were still common then, and pronghorn antelope also grazed the surrounding plain. Grizzly bears and coyotes abounded, and gray wolves were even reported. Wild horses— the progeny of escaped Spanish stock—had established themselves long before Fremont visited; "we found plenty of mustangs, wild horses, in 1807 . . . ," recounted Felipe Santiago Garcia, "and lots of mission cattle."

The entry of European livestock signaled a major, irreversible, but often unnoticed alteration of the basin's character. Today wild oats, European foxtail, Bermuda grass, and bur clover are simply assumed to be common regional flora, but botanist Beecher Crampton points out that those weeds and grasses, among many others, were transported in packing material, in the soil surrounding cuttings, in ship ballast, and, most important, in and on domestic animals, which were walking seed bags. As a result, even the Yokuts' usually benign practice of burning areas of dry prairie grasses to encourage earlier sprouting of the next crop actually helped hardy European annual weeds and grasses to replace natives.

By 1833, trapper Zenas Leonard observed that indigenous perennial bunchgrasses had been almost totally replaced. Consequences of that alteration were considerable, for this had been one of the world's great natural rangelands; both antelope and elk had depended upon bunchgrasses, so the natural web that included the ungulates was upset and their survival was threatened. By 1977, with antelope and elk long gone and most of the prairie gone too, another botanist, Harold Heady, suggested that "alien species should be considered as new and permanent members of the grassland rather than as aliens." This successful intrusion, of course, parallels the human dominance of European immigrants over the few remaining Yokuts.

Another major change occurred when farmers began diverting the lake's feeder streams for irrigation. At that point the large but fragile pool began to shrink significantly. Twenty years later, the first of many reclamation districts was composed and initiated the process of opening to farming what had previously been lake bed: "as the waters vanished, speculators and settlers stampeded to Kings County," states a 1913 history of the region. Farmers no longer had to wait for the summer dry-up to plant there.

As geographer Preston points out, "reclamation abruptly terminated the lake's traditional role as habitat for migratory fowl." It also abruptly terminated the lake itself—even the idea of it in the minds of most people. Its fishery had been destroyed; its resident beavers and otters were gone; its grizzlies and elk decimated; its remaining water impounded in a large evaporation pool and considered too salty to be of use. Ironically, the former lake bed would soon have to be irrigated.

Little of what was once natural in this basin has been saved. Great agricultural productivity has been gained, but there is deep irony that this once wildly diverse section of California strikes outsiders as homogeneous—fields and towns and roads that look too much alike. As novelist A. T. Bezzerides wrote in *Long Haul* (1938), one drives on, "passing through the small towns, Fowler and Kingsburg, Goshen and Pixley, town after town, Famosa and Bakersfield, mixing them up, thinking one was the other." The old lake bed now resembles nothing more than exactly what it has become, a grid of agribusiness.

27

Viewing the basin from an airplane, however, reveals the unerasable impress of sinuous, disorderly shores that were once edged by a miles-wide band of tules; the old lake's shadow is still distinctly there—however divided, however settled, however drained and irrigated—waiting for the next wet year. On it has been imposed the world's largest and most productive agricultural chessboard: what geographer Alvin Urquhart describes as geometry of ownership replacing geography of nature. But when nature provides more water than storage facilities can handle, the lake rises like a wet phoenix from the supine countryside—geography reasserts itself.

In 1969, for instance, the Kings River overflowed levees and suddenly Tulare Lake was again among the state's largest. Nine years later, following another generous spring runoff, the non-existent lake covered some 70 square miles of land—a far cry from the 780 it once enveloped but enough to disturb farmers. Another of the levees keeping water out of the lake's old bed was breached in 1983, and 30,000 acres of cropland were suddenly inundated.

That year the local irrigation district immediately sought permission to pump the offending water over the divide into the San Joaquin River, but there was a complication: white bass, an introduced, voracious predator of the young of game fish, infested the lake's latest reincarnation. If allowed into the San Joaquin's drainage, they might destroy its native fishery.

The following October, Tulare Lake's ghost was still there and the Corps of Engineers issued a permit for growers to pump their land dry, but required that fish screens be employed. Only twenty-four hours after the operation began, white bass were gillnetted downstream in the San Joaquin River, and pumping had to be halted. Then, reports Marc Reisner in *Cadillac Desert* (1986):

Fish and Game—as if to underscore the catastrophic consequences of releasing white bass—poured a thousand gallons of rotenone, a virulent pesticide, into six miles of river around the fish screen. . . . A week later, Fish and Game performed a second mass poisoning.

Eventually, despite urgent legal efforts by sportsmen's groups and environmentalists to stop them, growers were again allowed to pump the nonexistent lake into the river, and even today no one is certain if that action may have doomed the Sacramento-San Joaquin Delta's rich fishery. Playing with nature is rarely without cost.

Meanwhile, many local residents, their bottomland conveniently pumped dry, once more forgot the persistent lake, but some future wet winter it will be back to remind them. It will be back.

The special ecological and geographic distinctions that once defined Tulare Lake have been obscured by diversion of its major feeder streams, by the draining of its wetlands, and by the agricultural development of the basin; as a result, many people who live in the area today are themselves unaware of its distinctiveness. They never saw that great sheet of water, those miles of tules, those uncountable waterfowl, and they cannot imagine them. In their experience, this has always been furrowed farmland, crossed by tractors and irrigated along shimmering rows. Lake? What lake?

▼

"Tulare Lake," I repeat, not resisting the impulse to smile. "It doesn't exist."

This is just occult enough a statement to satisfy Carlos, so he says, "Far . . . out . . . ," stretching the words.

After one more long look at history, I pull the car back onto the interstate and continue our journey, glancing more than a driver should at Tulare Lake's latest reincarnation.

We leave the freeway at Seventh Standard Road and drive east. On one side an oil pump bows to us as we pass an inundated cotton field while, on the other, an isolated storm cloud trails tendrils of rain like a dark jellyfish in the sky. Well ahead— our perspectives distorted by angle and distance and crisp air— we glimpse the roofs and dark tree-clusters of Oildale, with steam plumes rising from the petroleum workings in the creased hills beyond. To the south, Bakersfield slopes on river bluffs.

Finally, as the road emerges from a stretch of orchards into open fields once more, I spy an irrigator, his legs encased in rubber boots that sag like a hippo's thick feet. He stands with hands cupping a smoke, leaning on a shovel, and he too surveys the distant glistening of a lake long dead. He waves as we pass and I give him thumbs up, then turn and smile at my son. Grandma and Grandpa's house is just ahead.

The Water Game

J OHN PHOENIX is acknowledged to have been one of
the West's first great humorists. Phoenix was actually the
nom de plume of a mischievous and talented graduate of
West Point, George Horatio Derby. A topographical engineer
for the United States Army, Derby wrote hilarious sketches
even while on military assignments. In 1849, however, when
he was dispatched to survey the Great Central Valley's farming
potential, the wag turned grim.

The area north of Fresno—now the richest agricultural

31

county in America—he reported, was "exceedingly barren, and singularly destitute of resources, except for a narrow strip on the borders of the stream; it was without timber and grass, and can never, in my estimation, be brought into requisition for agricultural purposes." Near present-day Bakersfield, in Kern County (the nation's second most productive), he found "the most miserable country that I ever beheld."

That same parched vale is now the most abundant agricultural cornucopia in the history of the world. Last year it produced over $15 billion in agriculture. How was that transformation possible? Distinguished historian W. H. Hutchinson says there were three principal reasons: "Water, water, and *more* water."

The control and manipulation of water in the arid West has been the key to everything from economics to politics here. Without water projects, there would be few Idaho potatoes; without water projects, little Arizona cotton, no Utah alfalfa. There would also be no Phoenix, no Las Vegas, and no Los Angeles—not as we know them, anyway. There would be no Reno or El Paso or Albuquerque either, because they too have grown up in desiccated areas.

The American West is, in the main, arid to semiarid land. But the natural beauty and value of arid land have rarely been apparent to people whose ancestors migrated from green Europe, so enormous amounts of money have been spent and rapacious bureaucracies created in an effort to "make the desert bloom." Although only a tiny portion of the land has so far been "developed," that has bloomed abundantly.

Unfortunately, these efforts have also produced the seeds of their own doom: problems such as soil salinization, compaction, and subsidence; the leaching and concentrating of natural toxins from previously dry earth; the overuse of agricultural chemicals, which in turn concentrate in the environment; and the devastation of once huge aquifers in order to flood-irrigate crops better suited to other climates in other places. These developments now seem to have placed Westerners on a path trod by Assyrians, Mesopotamians, and Aztecs, desert peoples who also once challenged nature—and failed.

In the past year, ten photographers have embarked on a project to dramatize this long-ignored environmental crisis. "We've been managing water as an abstract legal right or a commodity," points out Robert Dawson, the Californian who initiated the endeavor, "rather than the most basic physical source of life. We believe that water is misused nationwide. We're focusing on the arid West because development here stands in high relief against the vast, open landscape. It's here that the impact of technology, government, and human ambition is most visible." Many major water policy decisions remain to be made, and only an informed public can do that.

Nowhere are the gains and losses associated with water manipulation more obvious than in Dawson's home region, the Great Central Valley of California, the physical and economic core of our richest state. All significant cities here, the state's heartland, grew near watercourses; it is an oasis civilization.

But it isn't the existence of cities that makes this area vital. It is the fact that 25 percent of all table food produced in the United States is grown in this single valley.

The climate here seems close to perfect for farming. Following a short, splendid spring, an extended summer develops. Sun prevails and the horizon seems to expand. Thanks to water pumped or imported, the list of crops grown in this natural hothouse is continually expanding as new varieties are planted: exotic herbs and condiments this year, kiwi fruit and frost-free berries next. Meanwhile, native plants are rare and native animals—pronghorns, grizzlies, and condors—stand stuffed in local museums.

33

Here, too, a largely Hispanic work force toils on great farms owned by corporations, because this remains a place where the poor of any background can at least try to escape the cycle of poverty, one generation laboring that another might take advantage of the region's rich promise. But it isn't an easy climb; there has tended to be a direct link between centralized irrigation systems and centralized political and economic power, and that in turn has created a paternalistic, class-ridden society with nonwhites on the bottom.

Modern agribusiness is competitive, and Valley farmers and ranchers have been notable in inventing such agricultural devices as special adaptations of the clamshell dredge, peach defuzzers, olive pitters, wind machines to fight frost, hydraulic platforms for pruning, pneumatic tree-shakers for bringing down the fruit and nuts—a technological nascence of amazing creativity. But none of them would mean much without imported or pumped water.

Many farmers date their entry into Valley agriculture to the period just after World War I when the unregulated pumping of groundwater allowed fields to burgeon. Eventually farmers were pumping more and more from wells that had to be drilled deeper and deeper into unreplenishable aquifers. When the Central Valley Project and the California State Water Project— the two largest and most complex irrigation systems on earth— were completed, it seemed that at last the tapping of irreplaceable groundwater in the Valley could cease.

Today, more than 1,200 dams have been built, and thousands of miles of canals cross this onetime desert. Even that hasn't stopped subsurface pumping; it has actually expanded since those huge stores of surface water became available. Pumping now exceeds replenishment by more than half a *trillion* gallons annually, while ecosystems hundreds of miles to the north are threatened by the diversion of their rivers and creeks.

Writer Wallace Stegner has suggested that this area's—and by analogy, the West's—agriculture may have "to shrink back to something like the old, original scale, and maybe less than the original scale because there isn't the groundwater there anymore. It's actually more desert than it was when people first began to move in." Hutchinson adds, "We have to stop pretending we're frontiersmen dealing with unlimited water. There's too damn many of *us* and too damned little of *it*."

Giant agribusinesses in the Valley can buy that water for less than $10 per acre-foot, while northern California householders have paid well over $1,000 for the same acre-foot—with the difference subsidized by taxpayers. It seems to critics that such water is too cheap to use wisely and that both hubris and ignorance are manifest in the illusion that moisture unused by humans is somehow squandered, the natural world be damned—and dammed. Ironically, most people—including most Westerners—seem to prefer not to be aware of all this, lest salads and beef suddenly become more expensive.

Irrigation is big business, and both of the vast water projects in California were justified, in part at least, as measures that would save existing family farms and perhaps increase the number of acres cultivated by small farmers. In fact, both have led to more and more acres coming under cultivation by huge corporations—Chevron U.S.A., Prudential Insurance Company, Shell Oil Company, Southern Pacific Railroad, J. G. Boswell Company, Getty Oil, among others.

How has the quest for water changed the West? Last year, driving in the southwest corner of the Central Valley, I decided to investigate Buena Vista Lake where I'd fished when I was a boy. I crossed the California Aqueduct, then drove west and finally stopped the car. An immense agricultural panorama opened before me, cultivated fields of various hues extending in all directions.

All its tributary streams have been diverted and its bed is now dry, so, ironically, Buena Vista Lake must be irrigated. As I gazed at this scene, a red-tailed hawk wheeled overhead, riding a thermal. Far to the east a yellow tractor shimmered through heat waves like a crawdad creeping across the old lake's floor. I saw no dwellings, few trees.

That hawk swung far over a green field where tiny fingers of water from elsewhere glistened through rows and where a lone brown man, an irrigator, leaned on a shovel.

Welcome to the real West, where agribusiness executives in corporate boardrooms, not cowboys or Indians or even irrigators, are the principle players.

The Kern, My River

I N NOVEMBER of 1950, thirteen years old, I rode a city
bus that was escorted across a Kern River bridge by police.
Brown water full of logs and branches, even what appeared to
be parts of cabins, roiled beneath—and not very far beneath—
water higher than I'd ever seen. On the upstream side, teams
of men were working tensely with pike poles, trying to keep
flotsam from piling against the bridge. Even within the moving coach, I could feel the span quivering as we crossed into
Oildale. All traffic was halted shortly after my bus reached the
north side.

A pal named Floyd and I left it and joined others on a levee—
the top of which was eventually lapped with water—to observe
the drama. The day was overcast but not wet, so this scene
seemed unreal, like a movie. I finally grasped the reality of
events, however, when I saw a large pine tree rushing downstream with a lone, soaked jackrabbit mounted on its barren
trunk like a hood ornament. A moment later, the pine seemed
to explode as it hit the bridge, then somehow it emerged on the
other side, the rabbit still clinging to it.

Floyd, who had moved from Arkansas only a year earlier,
asked a question that hadn't even dawned on me: "How come
it to flood when it's not rainin'?" Many towns in the otherwise
dry Central Valley developed on the banks of rivers flowing
from the Sierra Nevada, and many of us born and raised there
simply assumed the rush of those icy streams as we assumed the
pulsing of our own blood. "I don't know," I replied, blinking.

Six years later, John Takeuchi and I hiked from Quaking
Aspen into Forks of the Kern where the large North Fork—
the river's main channel—is joined by Little Kern River, a
stream small enough for us to wade. We were nearly a hundred
miles above Oildale in what is now called the Golden Trout
Wilderness. We were also at the source of that 1950 flood.

A terrific storm had occurred on the Little Kern, which in
turn engorged the North Fork, itself already running high.
Downstream, near the old town of Kernville, the South Fork
contributed more water to the swollen stream, and every mountain creek along its steep journey south added runoff until a
torrent plunged down the narrow canyon of the lower Kern, de-
stroying cabins, uprooting trees, drowning squirrels and lizards
alike. It peaked at a tremendous 42,000 cubic feet of muddy
water per second, some ten times its normal flow at that time
of year, bursting from mountains near Bakersfield like a desert
flash flood, engulfing bottomland, reclaiming ancient chan-

nels, some long forgotten. In Bakersfield, where many streets were lower than the streambed, levees had been constructed to control just such surges and, fortunately, no major breaches occurred. But Buena Vista Lake near Taft suddenly occupied thousands of additional acres and much cultivated land was inundated with water from distant mountains.

The Kern River may be California's most interesting stream. The state's third-longest, it flows approximately 164 miles from the high plateau west of Mount Whitney to erstwhile wetlands south and west of Bakersfield. During extremely wet years such as 1862, however, its waters surged north another 250 miles to San Francisco Bay via Buena Vista Slough, Tulare Lake, and the San Joaquin River's drainage. While its flow has been diminished by weirs and canals channeling it for irrigation, the Kern still traverses more mountain mileage than any other Sierran stream, emerging onto flatland at Kern Canyon's mouth after a journey of some 120 miles. It is also the only major stream to run south rather than west, plunging through two gorges as it splits the range. Reputed to be one of California's best trout streams as well as the most dangerous river in the state, the Kern concomitantly provides some of the finest raftable white water in North America.

In one sense, Kern River now stands as a symbol for all of California's once-wild streams: harnessed, directed, and utilized but not fully tamed. It retains an edge of wildness— the capacity for an occasional flash flood and more than an occasional drowning. Human history is tied to it and human intervention has in places changed it beyond recognition. This river has, for instance, contributed mightily to the San Joaquin Valley's agricultural richness, depositing over the millennia thousands of acres of rich alluvial soil; now it irrigates many of those same acres.

To me, however, raised on its banks, it was simply "the

river," the southern boundary of my parched hometown. A riparian forest lined the stream and, beyond that greenery, horned toads and jackrabbits and ants rested in the thin shade of tumbleweeds, while summer heat bent light into wet-looking waves. But always, as certain as sky and breath, those huge cottonwoods, those willows, those mysterious hanging vines, always those currents of chilled, crystalline water: Like most kids raised in Oildale, my life braided with the Kern, entwined with an intimacy that now seems extraordinary. I swam in its dangerous and forbidden waters, fished its pools and runs, explored on its wooded banks, attended the funerals of two friends who drowned in it. I ate food irrigated by it, drank its water, and stood mourning when its forest died and its bed became a sandy desert. I called it "the river," but thought of it as *mine*, my river.

Kern River water begins its long downstream journey among snowbanks and rills on the western slopes of Mt. Whitney, and descends through canyons and meadows to the Great Central Valley, traversing many major habitats as it drops. Its genesis can be found on a high granite plateau, 10,000 to 11,000 feet above sea level. That glaciated realm is starkly beautiful with tarns, moraines, and spectacular hanging valleys on both east and west sides, while spongy alpine meadows and trees decorate the slopes. At 10,700 feet, on a secondary path connecting the John Muir trail with the Kern River trail, an unnamed lake offers spectacular views of nearby peaks. It also constitutes the first puddling of what will be the Kern River—water which one day might lap levees in Oildale. The North Fork ultimately provides 85 percent of the Kern River's annual 700,000 acre-feet of water, and 80 percent of that will be accumulated from snowpack in the first fifteen miles of its channel, so it is a high-mountain river indeed.

Wandering that distant alpine realm offers a powerful antidote for the malaise of modern life. Mountaineer Thomas Winnett writes: "This stretch of country composes the least visited, least known and least trampled region in the southern Sierra." It feels as remote as another person's dreams, but this area has by no means been unapproachable: When Clarence King crossed here in 1873, he noted: "The Kern Plateau, so green and lovely on my former visit . . . was now a gray sea of rolling granite ridges, darkened at intervals by forest, but no longer velveted with meadows and upland grasses. The indefatigable shepherds have camped everywhere, leaving hardly a spear of grass behind them."

Those alpine meadows, protected by statute, no longer must endure sheep and cattle. Their streams and lakes are the ancestral home to lustrous Golden Trout (*Salmo aguabonita*), a species now much transplanted but originally unique to the Kern drainage. A resident subspecies, the Kern River Rainbow (*Salmo gardnerira gilberti*), is a favorite of fishermen. Because of this area's remoteness, another, endangered subspecies, the Greenback Cutthroat trout (*Salmo clarki*), has been transplanted here from its vulnerable Rocky Mountain habitat.

In 1889 a party of mountaineers from Bakersfield made their way to Mount Whitney. On August 13, they reached the upper Kern, which, "for twenty-five miles coursed due north and south cutting through the very heart of the Sierras. Lofty mountains arose on either hand, and the trail which of necessity hugged closely to the river bed, passed from one to another charming little flat densely timbered with living and fallen giants." The twenty-five-mile stretch "cutting through the very heart of the Sierras" is actually one of the most remarkable environs of the Sierra Nevada, a U-shaped valley called the Kern Trench down which the river slices. It resembles an unspoiled Yosemite or Hetch Hetchy, with a gentle, steady southward slope and relatively verdant vegetation because of a longer growing season than is typical of the surrounding alpine country.

This microenvironment, 2,000 to 5,000 feet below surrounding ridges, follows an ancient earthquake rift—Kern Canyon fault—that has been in the process of being deepened and widened by rushing water for, geologists estimate, 30,000,000 years. During the Ice Age, it was cleansed and shaped by the vast Kern Glacier, which is given most credit for the trough's symmetrical shape. As it gouged south, it also left smaller valleys that channeled tributary creeks hanging high above on granite walls, water dangling down those walls as though desperate. It is not entirely stable geologically, as is illustrated by the birth of Kern Lake in 1867, when a massive landslide in the trench dammed the river and formed a large, marshy lagoon that remains a landmark near the deep canyon's southern end.

That episode illustrates once more something that few residents in the dry Central Valley truly comprehended: Events so far away can cataclysmically impact them. Despite days of steady rain as Christmas approached in 1867, Kern River's bed near Bakersfield went mysteriously dry, an ominous occurrence indeed. Finally much of the water built up behind the vast natural dam in the distant, upstream trench burst free, and the greatest flood on record exploded from Kern Canyon. So powerful was it that the river's channel in the valley was permanently altered from a southern course to the route that eventually demarcated Oildale, a bed eighteen feet *higher* than much of Bakersfield. Construction on a levee system was begun there immediately.

In the high country far from human fears, the North Fork leaves the Kern Trench, veers south past Grasshopper Camp and beyond Hole in the Ground, southeast into a tight, disorderly section of cascades and rapids called Hells (*sic*) Hole.

42

Here can be found a beautiful, aromatic campsite called Cedars of Hells Hole that has been a favorite of packers and hikers alike for nearly a century. Continuing its turbulent course, the river then plunges into narrows, reaching an explosive cataract called Kern Falls. The stream continues gushing south into another narrow canyon. It calms again as it reaches a large meadow called Kern Flat, where the aluminum remains of a crashed airplane have rested, a mute monument, for forty years. The current once more picks up velocity as it swerves southwest toward the Forks, where it will merge with the Little Kern—a stream that might more accurately be called the West Fork.

There is another flat here, and in 1855 miners, 5,000 of them living in tents and hovels, assembled in this remote locale for a mini gold rush. It soon turned bust, however, and by winter the hopefuls had scattered. One contemporary described the disintegrating camp this way: "Provisions, tools, bad whiskey and vicious rattlesnakes in all directions." Rusting machinery can still be found at this location near a seeping salt springs.

Thanks to a spate of road building in the 1960s, the Forks is now only two miles from the nearest parking area. This setting is popular with campers, since the Little Kern is a pleasant and safe stream and the North Fork produces big trout in abundance each year. River rafters in particular enjoy the challenge presented on the merged, fourteen-and-a-half-mile downstream section through another granite canyon that extends south to Johnsondale Bridge. A spokesman for Kern River Tours called this "the most demanding white-water run in California," and it is indeed a roiling, rowdy series of rapids and waves—class five plus—that burst over paddlers' heads. In 1987, this pristine segment of the Kern was granted National Wild and Scenic River status.

At Johnsondale Bridge, the river reaches a road for the first time. From here south to Kernville, twenty-six miles, there are six Forest Service Camps plus many private resorts and cabins and, on major holidays such as Memorial Day and Labor Day, as many as 40,000 recreationalists—most of them from the megalopolis in Southern California—may flock to what was once a remote river. Present-day Kernville, which old-timers call New Kernville, is situated downstream at the head of a wide basin known as Kern Valley.

This natural bowl and its environs were the scene of a gold rush between 1855 and 1858, centered at Keyesville, the first town in Kern County. In 1861, a man named Lovely Rogers found a rich lode in a nearby canyon, reportedly while searching for a lost mule. This became the famous Big Blue Mine and a town called Rogersville sprang up around the diggings. Soon a local temperance society managed to impose a ban on all alcoholic beverages there. Two years later, enterprising Adam Hamilton began another settlement, this one called Whiskey Flat, a mile downriver. Guess which one prospered! Whiskey Flat's citizens later changed its name to Kernville, and it eventually became the area's principal community.

When I was a kid, my folks often visited that community— natives refer to it as Old Kernville—a tree-lined town that featured a beautiful river-stone hotel near the rushing stream. I recognized that building the first time I ever glimpsed it because I had seen it frequently in class-B westerns filmed in this picturesque setting; it was much favored by moviemakers. The basin in which the town rested always seemed green indeed after the tans and browns of Oildale; it was full of cattle and farms.

The North Fork used to run through the center of Old Kernville, but today the townsite and river channel are no longer visible—they were inundated when a lake filled there in 1954 following the completion of Isabella Dam. Residents were relocated upstream on higher ground to New Kernville, a scenic locale where I had often fished for trout. Now the entire southern end of Kern Valley is a lake bed, the stream dammed to the south before it plunges into Lower Kern Canyon for its final rush toward the Great Central Valley.

Isabella's main dam is 185 feet high and 1,725 feet long and its reservoir covers fourteen square miles, storing 550,000 acre-feet of water. It has aided in flood control, its raison d'être; there have been no more significant deluges since it was constructed—and there had better not be, since houses have now been built on the Kern's floodplain downstream near Bakersfield. It has helped Central Valley farmers as well by regulating and guaranteeing year-round water for irrigation. It also provided a coup de grace to seasonal wetlands that once characterized the area around Bakersfield.

East of the dam, the South Fork of the Kern flows into Isabella Lake. Shortly before reaching the large pool that now covers the place where it historically merged with the North Fork, this brisk stream passes through the Nature Conservancy's Kern River Preserve, which protects the largest contiguous cottonwood-and-willow woodland remaining in California, a jungle of riverine greenery in the midst of dry scenery. Vegetation is lush, and the profligacy of bird and other animal life there is astounding—a glimpse of an earlier, natural California.

That same territory was once the residence of a small, secluded Shoshonean tribe, the Tubatulabal. Their isolated location allowed them to develop a unique and, to us, mysterious culture. They were not, however, mysterious to a soldier named Captain Moses McLaughlin. On the night of April 13, 1863—long after white farmers had without incident established themselves in the area—just east of the site of Isabella Dam near Wofford Heights, McLaughlin ordered his troops to surround a Tubatulabal village and attack it. They met little resistance.

"Killed thirty-five of them," his official report boasted. "Not a soldier was injured." Survivors who couldn't hide were rounded up by troops and herded to a reservation at Fort Tejon, nearly seventy-five miles away in the Tehachapi Mountains. Patti Wermuth, whose great-great-grandmother escaped, says her ancestors were "very timid people. They didn't have a word for 'war' or 'peace.'" The village was never again populated, but downstream that same year, Thomas Baker set in motion the events that led to the development of Bakersfield. One community destroyed, another born.

Not far from where the Tubatulabal village once stood, mountain man Joseph R. Walker in 1845 guided "the Pathfinder," John Charles Frémont, and his band into Kern Valley. Frémont named the river he found there—"the swiftest stream we have crossed since leaving the bay"—after the chief artist and topographer of his party, Edward M. Kern, perhaps because the latter almost drowned trying to cross it. He did not know that in 1776, the first European to cross the river, Padre Francisco Garces, had already named it Rio de San Felipe. Twenty-eight years later another priest, Padre Maria de Zalvidea, called it La Porciuncula (named, apparently, for the first Franciscan monastery in Italy, or perhaps for a religious holiday of the same name). But the most accurate title came from Hispanic settlers who began populating the region in significant numbers in the 1840s. They called it Rio Bravo, Wild River, and the term remains in common usage among some local folks.

In 1863, William Henry Brewer described the region below present-day Isabella Dam: "The spot is picturesque—the granite mountains are steep and high, and the Kern River runs through a wild, picturesque canyon." Below the dam, in the "wild" canyon, the river's flow is now regulated by the Army Corps of Engineers. Water slips into a narrow, rocky channel that used to froth white the year round, then into a deep cleft. Last summer, I telephoned a rafting company to arrange a trip on the twelve-mile section to Democrat Hot Springs. I was told, however, that the journey wasn't possible because "the Corps turned the water off." This section, mostly class three or four (intermediate) rapids, nonetheless contains what many regard as the most difficult stretch on the river, a class six-plus called the Royal Flush, around which rafts must be portaged. Chuck Richards of Whitewater Voyages calls it "the most savage and severe we've ever seen."

"The Kern was the last major river in California to be developed for river rafting," Richards explains. "It had sort of an 'unrunable' mystique to it. Maybe it was because of all the drownings." Maybe so. Although none have been rafting-related, 150 people have drowned since 1968 in the swift stretch of river between Isabella Dam and Rancheria Road at the mouth of the lower canyon. Seventeen drowned in 1986 alone—its deadliest year to date.

And each year, the Kern County Sheriff's Department is called on for seventy-five to one hundred rescues. Why is the Kern so dangerous? "Usually, there's a pool of water before the rapids and another below," explains Sergeant Charlie Church, supervisor of the Search and Rescue Squad. "The river drops so fast. You never know. There could be a torrent that pulls you into the rapids." Lieutenant Carl Sparks agrees. "It's the current. There's a hell of a undertow."

In the canyon where I frequently fished, near Hobo (now Miracle) Hot Springs, a short-lived but intense uranium boom occurred in 1954. For a while Geiger counters were sported like six-guns and, more than once while angling in what I thought were remote locations along the river, I encountered wary pros-

47

pectors. The cleft here is steep, and so is the river's drop as it curves through rocks. Little wonder then that the river's first hydroelectric operation—a small dam and turbine generator—was completed in 1890. There are now six power plants on the river.

Eventually the Kern slides from a deep, dramatic slash in brown mountains east of Bakersfield and enters flat land, where it has contributed not only to the birth of the Great Central Valley itself but also to the vast wetlands that into this century characterized the Valley's southern end. As it levels, the river still surges powerfully and its rocky bed becomes increasingly sandy with ground granite. This is a deceptive stretch, where each year many drownings occur. Wrote Brewer in 1863, "Kern River is a wide swift stream here, about twenty or twenty-five rods wide, with a treacherous, sandy bottom." A hundred and twenty-five years later, a ninety-year-old vaquero, Arnold "Chief" Rojas, agreed, "Oh, yeah, we used to hate trailing cattle across that river. It was so swift and there was quicksand. *Muy peligroso!*"

Not far from the mouth of Kern Canyon, on May 1, 1776—not quite two months before the Declaration of Independence was signed—Padre Francisco Garces, a Spaniard from Aragon, became the first European known to have visited the Kern. Accompanied by two Mojave guides, he arrived at a Yokuts village where he saw "a great river which made much noise. . . ." The Indians, whom he described as "affable and affectionate," feted him.

When it came time to leave, "They asked me if I knew how to swim, and I answered them 'nay.'" The Yokuts then "ordered me to undress, which I did, down to shirt and drawers. They insisted that I should put off every garment but this I refused to do. They convoyed me across between four of them by swimming."

48

The arrival of Padre Garces symbolized the beginning of the end of the Yokuts' world. Theodora Kroeber and Robert Heizer describe them as "the ultimate realization of Heartland people in features and form, in the extreme rounding of face and body and in temperament that fitted the ample curves like a second skin." Alfred Kroeber points out that this large, regionally dominant group (perhaps as many as 40,000) was one of the few California cultures that divided into true tribes; their home "was the San Joaquin Valley, the entire floor of which they held," as well as areas of surrounding foothills. Unfortunately, diseases such as Spanish influenza, cholera, smallpox, whooping cough, and syphilis decimated them and considerably weakened their power to resist the commandeering of their homeland by whites.

Today, the Kern River becomes liquid gold when it reaches the Valley's floor, where it is employed to irrigate some of the richest farms in the world. Asserts historian Donald Worster, "The technological control of water was the basis of a new West," and this stream has been no exception. Back in 1954, when Isabella Dam was built far upriver, there were serious questions about why the natural flow was blocked and what the consequences would be. Ardis Walker of Kernvilles Old and New, served on the County Board of Supervisors at that time, and he suggests, "Agricultural interests promoted the dam as flood control but actually they took control of the water. Big industrial farmers call the shots on when it goes down and how much goes where." As it does so many other things in Kern County, agribusiness dominates water politics. Gail Schontzler wrote in the *Bakersfield Californian*:

Where did all the water go?

That question is often asked by newcomers to Bakersfield who drive by the Kern River and see nothing but a big sand lot.

The answer is that nearly all the water is owned by farmers. For many months of the year the riverbed is sucked dry to irrigate crops.

Some of those "farmers" are large corporations. Their "farms" run to tens of thousands of acres and they employ not only tractor drivers and irrigators but teams of lawyers and well-placed lobbyists. In Kern County agriculture is big business indeed.

When Thomas Baker arrived in this region it was known as Kern Island, three major distributary channels of the river surrounding what would one day be Bakersfield. Those fingers of water eventually drained into 4,000-acre Buena Vista Lake to the west and 8,300-acre Kern Lake to the south, both of which waxed in the spring and waned in the fall like great vernal pools. Tule marshes and sloughs connected the two and, during wet years, linked them to vast Tulare Lake to the north. All this in an arid land that welcomed only six inches of rain annually.

The historic relationship of land and water and wealth hereabouts is illustrated by a tale that merges Kern River history and folklore. First the history: In 1850, Congress passed the Swamp and Overflow Act, which granted various states the title to what was deemed valueless, waterlogged land. Such parcels became unavailable to homesteaders and tended to be sold to established landholders. Conditions in California were not well understood then, so the act contributed mightily to the development of Bakersfield when Baker and Harvey Brown undertook the reclamation of 400,000 acres. Much of that acreage was boggy only during the rainy season or in especially wet years. During the drought of 1864, much of the land had "reclaimed" itself and, under terms of the act, Baker personally acquired 87,120 acres. Little wonder he could allow travelers to rest in his "field."

Now the folklore: One of the genuine moguls of the late nineteenth century, a resourceful German immigrant named Henry Miller, of Miller and Lux, is reported to have hitched teams of horses to a boat and had himself pulled about over a vast, dry tract so he could swear, when claiming it as wetland, that he had navigated it by boat. While distinguished historian W. H. Hutchinson winks at that story, he does confirm that the region's agricultural diversity "stems from the variety of favorable soils and climates—plus always *irrigation.*"

Henry Miller figured in the major historical event involving Kern River irrigation rights. In 1881, the case of *Lux v. Haggin* was tried, a battle of agribusiness goliaths which actually pitted the company of Miller and his partner, Charles Lux, against James Ben Ali Haggin and Lloyd Tevis, who in 1890 would incorporate as the Kern County Land Company. The outcome of the suit would decide water rights in California for decades to come. Miller and Lux owned fifty miles along both sides of the Kern and had built a one-hundred-foot-wide canal to carry water to other holdings. Trouble arose when Haggin and Tevis bought land upstream and filed claims for use of the water. The suit weighed Miller and Lux's "riparian rights"—rights of streamside landholders, mostly ranchers, to take whatever water they wanted—against Haggin and Tevis's "appropriation rights" to divert upstream water to distant farms.

Five years later, after Haggin and Company had won in a lower court, a Supreme Court justice performed what historian Carey McWilliams described as "a curious flip-flop," and a split decision upheld Miller and Lux's riparian right—or privilege—establishing the "California Doctrine." Ultimately Miller and Haggin compromised, but the doctrine endured until 1928, a lawyer's dream—or nightmare. Complex to the point of being knotty, it nonetheless made one thing clear: Farmers who did not own river frontage might go without. That, in turn, led to both greater reliance on pumps for underground supplies and one of the nineteenth century's most important pieces of agricultural legislation, the Irrigation District Act of 1887, which allowed farmers to cooperatively build and operate watering systems in the thirsty Valley. This, in turn, gave smaller landholders a means to compete against the Henry Millers and the James Ben Ali Haggins.

Many things are interrelated when it comes to this river and water usage in Kern County. Pumping, for instance, depletes groundwater so river flow is diverted to replenish the aquifer, creating a water bank for future usage. Early in the 1980s, another, minor version of the old Miller-Lux vs. Haggin-Tevis battle occurred. George W. Nickel, Jr. (grandson of Henry Miller) accused Tenneco West (modern incarnation of Kern County Land Company) of pumping water that had been allowed to perk underground by the city of Bakersfield and the Olcese Water District—the latter served Nickel's Rio Bravo Tennis Ranch. To no one's surprise, Tenneco denied it. Reported the *Bakersfield Californian*: "While Nickel criticizes Tenneco, his own use of the Kern River has also come under scrutiny." Business as usual in Kern County, it seems, since this is only one of many battles over local water rights.

Another business has contributed mightily to this region's economy. In 1899, James Elwood and his father, Jonathon, struck oil sand after digging only thirteen feet with a simple auger-drill on the Kern River's bank near Gordon's Ferry just north of Bakersfield. Here the channel swings beneath a high bluff known as China Grade and oil seeps had long been noted. A full-fledged well was completed and within five years the Kern River Oil Field was the state's most productive. It remains a major producer.

That industry brought my parents to Oildale, a town that grew early in this century on the stream's northern bank. It was originally an adjunct of the Kern River Field, a rough enclave of single males. Recalls noted author Lawrence Clark Powell, who worked in the area as a youth in 1919, "We quickly learned to avoid Oildale, thank you."

Oildale was, in any case, a fine, lively place to come of age, and growing up there led me in 1945 to the handlebars of Wally Coleman's bicycle. He was the neighborhood pal who first showed me "the jungle" that lined Kern River. Wally would also be my first close friend to drown in the river a few years later. We kids used to pedal our bikes over dirt roads and trails across barren tracts to the incongruously lush riverine forest, full of birds and scurrying animals, hanging vines, impenetrable thickets, myriad sliding channels.

But the construction of Isabella Dam and the increased diversion of water for agriculture changed all that by ending seasonal floods and allowing total cessation of downstream flow to Oildale for most of the year. By the mid-1950s, I was driving to the jungle to park with girlfriends. I didn't at first notice, let alone understand, the consequences of diminished downstream water, but within two years of the dam's completion, the lush riverine forest began to die.

The demise of that rich woodland near Oildale actually indicated another, deeper loss. Recent research by ecologists and biologists has considerably enlarged the concept of what a river is: A rich world of shrimps, worms, insects, and other microscopic organisms has been discovered living in groundwater below stream channels and sometimes for great distances on each side. "River ecologists have traditionally dealt with what the eye can see," points out Garth Redfield of the National Science Foundation, "but we may have been ignoring one of the most important components of a river system—what is happening underground." Subterranean aquatic organisms are integral to a food chain that extends all the way to large fish and

53

animals that prey on them—including anglers. Once ground-water organisms die, rehydrating a channel will not soon restore the complex ecological web. By 1960, when I returned home from the army, both the forest and the underground river that supported it were dead.

Late last August, fifty-two years after I was born along one of the river's old channels, I jogged across what had been our jungle—now dusty bridle trails, grotesque, desiccated snags. The great cottonwoods and willows, the sprawling vines of wild grapes, are dead and dried like unwrapped mummies; wood-peckers, tree frogs, and scurrying squirrels are gone, all gone, and so, in Oildale, is the river itself as a living thing. Stream diversion and a collapsed water table have completely destroyed them. I can only mourn for the river, my river, and for the generation in my hometown that has grown up without ever knowing it.

Still running, I followed a bike path on the southern levee, a canal at my left side carrying water deflected and rechanneled from far upstream toward some farmers' fields while the wide riverbed on my right was arid. At Chester Avenue, I crossed a bridge to Oildale and halted mid-span. China Grade loomed east of me; Oildale sprawled in the north; Bakersfield crowded on the south. To the West, though, where I once saw a pine tree with a rabbit riding it disappear on a surge of brown water, I beheld only a ribbon of sand, wide and glaring, seeming to extend in the distance like the line of life itself. Far ahead, a lone rider and horse shimmering in heat waves crossed that narrow desert.

Then nothing moved but those chimerical waves.

California's
Literary Landscape

A T THE turn of this century, Theodore Roosevelt observed, "When I am in California, I am not in the
west, I am west of the west," but his view is suspect because he
didn't say *which* California and he didn't say *when*. Like many
outsiders, Roosevelt failed to recognize that there were—and
are—many Californias.

At the very time T.R. spoke, for instance, vaqueros and cowboys herded cattle over much of the San Joaquin Valley, the
Tehachapi Mountains, and the Diablo Range, while America's

last "wild Indian," Ishi, struggled to survive in foothills north-east of Sacramento, and miners still haunted the state's deserts and foothills. Loggers were clearing America's richest forests on the north coast. All those sections were the West, period.

But in Southern California then, a great real-estate boom, wedded to an increasingly romanticized version of the mission past, was churning. Hollywood was beginning its move from sleepy village to motion picture capital, producing a society that was indeed west of the West . . . west, perhaps, of any-thing. The very word "west" was beginning to take on new and bizarre connotations. And the San Francisco–Oakland Bay Area at that time was already a Pacific metropolis unlike any other in the United States: west of the West.

The real problem is that too many people—including some who claim to be experts—don't recognize that California is a collection of distinct regions, of unique histories and ex-periences, of varied people gathered under one name. It has no single homogeneous core—unless it is hope. As British writer Michael Davie observes, "California has been the ulti-mate frontier of the Western world: the stopping place of man's strange westering urge." To paraphrase poet Gary Snyder, the state is a fiction, but the regions are real. Actual people live in Huron or Susanville or El Monte—distinct locales—not in a mythical Golden State.

Ours is a diverse, dissident, distinct literature because ours is a diverse, dissident, and always distinctive society. For ex-ample, Davie also observed, "In California, the European trav-eler cannot fail to be struck by the absence of the political, social, and religious arrangements the rest of America derived from Europe." Contrast that with D. H. Lawrence's famed ob-servation, "California is a queer place . . . it has turned its back on the world, and looks into the void Pacific." The former is a statement about California; the latter is a statement about *Eurocentricism.*

In reality, of course, the vast and teeming Pacific is indeed a focus here, but so are Latin America and the Middle East and Asia and, yes, Europe, but the latter is not our preoccupation. Increasingly, we are developing a worldview that actually views the world. As a result, this is a place whose exotic components speak in new literary forms and about new possibilities. Look, for instance, at how many contemporary Californian writers of note are nonwhite, are women, are from working-class backgrounds. Look at how many are wackos. A richness of weather and geography and society influences both places and people here.

Although I'm a fifth-generation Californian, when I originally read *Rabbit Boss* and *The Loved One, The Maltese Falcon* and *The Day of the Locust,* they described terrains as alien to me as the far side of the moon. When I read *The Grapes of Wrath,* however, and *My Name is Aram* and *The Residual Years,* I was exploring the land of my heart, a rooted reality.

Each of us builds our own internal California, so in a sense there are as many variations as there are Californians. Any of us raised here can base our version of the state upon actual places and experiences. Those of us lucky enough also to be readers, of course, can allow authors to help us expand and sharpen our narrow personal variations of the state. It's clear, however, that even in this computer age 27 million subjective versions present far too cumbersome a collection to be of practical use.

Writer Bonnie Bruinslot has suggested that California is the Renaissance reincarnated, all the diversity of that age combined in space instead of time into a contemporary quilt. Most other scholars and editors have developed their own models allowing them to better understand the state's literary reality.

One classic scheme is to view the state as (a) the populous, trendy coastal strip and (b) everything else. In their classic collection, *California Heritage,* John and Laree Caughey employed a strictly chronological order with no regional references. So did W. Storrs Lee in *California, A Literary Chronicle.* Gary Soto in *California Childhood* used a tripartite regional division: Northern California, Central Valley, and Southern California. Mystery writer Frederick Zackel has urged a brutally pragmatic contemporary model: homeowners and non-homeowners. James D. Houston, on the other hand, suggests a more complex view: rural and urban writing viewed as separate categories and examined diachronically and synchronically—the categorization of specific locales altering as circumstances change.

I believe that four geo-literary zones and one exclusively imaginary realm have emerged from writing done here, each reflecting distinct history and literary outputs. The four are the Greater Bay Area, the Heartland (the state's rural regions, principally the Central Valley and the Salinas Valley), Wilderness California (the state's mountains, deserts, forests, and remaining wild coastline), and the Southland. My fifth section is called Fantasy California—the state as state of mind, the confusion of illusion with reality.

The concept of regions, of course, should be seen as an acknowledgment of the state's diversity rather than an iron-clad dictum. It's also clear that, thanks to modern mobility, many authors produce work set in more than one of these regions: Gary Snyder has made major contributions to both Bay Area and Wilderness California; Joan Didion's output includes books set in both the Heartland and the Southland, and she has even danced with the border of Fantasy California. In any case, those of us who live here recognize that there is more than one California.

The Greater Bay Area

San Francisco Bay allowed the development of a rough-hewn imitation of an eastern seaport, attracting to the region during the late 1840s and 1850s such estimable if largely forgotten authors (along with their signal noms de plume) as Alonzo Delano (Old Box), George Horatio Derby (John Phoenix), Louisa Smith Clapp (Dame Shirley), and John Rollin Ridge (Yellow Bird). The following decade—San Francisco was by 1860 the fourteenth-largest city in the Union—saw the development of a national literary reputation by writers operating in the San Francisco area, especially the Golden Gate Trinity (Bret Harte, Ina Coolbrith, and Charles Warren Stoddard, the three editors of the *Overland Monthly*), plus their partner, Mark Twain, a high in Western American letters. What was most important, perhaps, is that artists of the time reflected a distinctness still associated with the region; they believed themselves to be liberated from the East and from the Puritan past.

The Bohemian Club was founded in 1872 and for a while it actually included some bohemians. In fact, avant garde movements have continued to flourish on the North Coast. Late in the last century, for example, creative people began gathering at Carmel. Some, like Joaquin Miller, were links to the past; most, however, bespoke a new generation's dynamism: Jack London, Lincoln Steffens, George Sterling, Nora May French, Stoddard, Mary Hunter Austin, and a host of lesser-known writers.

By the early twentieth century, then, this had become one of America's most productive, most controversial literary regions. The North Coast's bohemians—up to and including Jack Kerouac and the Beats, Ken Kesey and his Merry Pranksters, Richard Brautigan and the Hippies, Jim Dodge (perhaps even Thomas Pynchon) and the North Coasters—have been everything from space cadets to geniuses.

The region now features a trendy mixture of urban sophistication and neo-savagery, of ecological concern in the midst of environmental despoilment. Gary Snyder captures those qualities in "Marin-An":

> . . . the twang
> of a pygmy nuthatch high in a pine—
> from behind the cypress windrow
> the mare moves up, grazing.
> a soft continuous roar
> comes out of the far valley
> of six-lane highway—thousands
> and thousands of cars
> driving men to work.

The Heartland

The Heartland has attracted an ethnically and socially diverse series of migrants to work in its fields. This region has typified the *real* California Dream, because virtually the only path to a better life for most emigrants has traditionally been hard physical labor. It has tended to attract the tough, the determined, possibly the desperate.

However, since the emergence of three Heartland natives—William Saroyan, William Everson, and John Steinbeck—in the 1930s, this section has produced a steady stream of innovative literature. Much of this writing starts with the soil, the physical reality from which so many people wrest their livings. Harsh rural realities have shaped much of the literature produced here, limiting much illusion without harming expression. Wilma McDaniel writes in "To the Point":

Hovis wore
a big black hat
pure Okie style
and him fourteen
The shed boss teased
Boy
did you steal your
daddy's hat
No sir
I worked all week
and bought me one.

A list of recent writers from this realm makes it clear that this region is now producing an extraordinary crop of native-born writers; best-known is that creative cluster known as the Fresno Poets.

Wilderness California

After a flying vulture had examined his supine body, the poet Robinson Jeffers wrote:

> . . . *how beautiful he looked, veering*
> *away in the sea-light over the precipice. I tell you*
> *solemnly*
> *I was sorry to have disappointed him. To be eaten*
> *By that beak and become part of him, to share those*
> *wings and those eyes—*
> *a sublime end of one's body, what an enskyment;*
> *What a life after death.*
>
> —"Vulture"

Outsiders don't always understand the dimensions of our state's undeveloped land, or the richness of our flora and fauna.

Pronghorns, elk, and grizzlies once teemed in the Central Valley, and great condors soared above it; all but elk are gone, and they survive only in a small reserve. But open land remains: the Mojave and Colorado deserts. The remarkable and varied coastline. Bigfoot country northwest; northeast, a volcanic moonscape. Moreover, California is spined by mountains: the Sierra Nevada, the Cascades, the Coast Ranges, the Tehachapis. All these places and their natural inhabitants have inspired writers.

Look, for example, at the literary reclamation of the desert. Those barren lands had once been crossed by pioneers too intent upon survival to notice the unique beauty surrounding them. By the turn of the century, however, the arid lands could be studied and sometimes romanticized. It was one of those interesting cases where changing circumstances allowed people to revision an area.

John C. Van Dyke's *The Desert* was in 1901 the first in a series of books that changed the way those ostensible wastelands were viewed. J. Smeaton Chase, Charles Fletcher Lummis, and George Wharton James also contributed important work, but the finest of all desert books, the most mystical and eloquent, is Mary Hunter Austin's *The Land of Little Rain*, published two years after Van Dyke's volume.

California's mountains and forests boast as distinguished a cadre of authors as do its deserts. The master here, of course, is John Muir. His work ranged from romantic to scientific. In books such as *The Mountains of California* or *My First Summer in the Sierra*, his prose soared toward poetry. Don't forget William Henry Brewer's delightful *Up and Down California, 1860–64*; when he wrote his notes, nearly all the state was still wilderness. Time remains important in this regional equation.

Sometimes ignored when considering Wilderness California

is its impact on poets and novelists, yet it has inspired some of the state's finest literature. For instance, much of Jeffers's remarkable poetry—say, "Roan Stallion"—demonstrates the symbolic power of California's coastline and hills. George R. Stewart wrote of Sierra forest when he produced two of his most memorable novels, *Storm* and *Fire,* and one of Walter Van Tilburg Clark's strongest and most magical novels, *The Track of the Cat,* is set in eastern Sierra cattle country. David Rains Wallace's *The Klamath Knot* is a contemporary treasure, Gary Snyder has set much recent poetry in the Sierra Nevada, and Ardis Walker explores the Kern Plateau in much of his poetry.

The Southland

And here upon this brazen hill
this hill above the aimless lights
I watch the always going home
the going west into the night.
the going towards two-bedroom flats
the going towards the blinding screen
the alcohol the marriage debts
the insane hours in between
the painful clock the cereal
the always sweating late at work
the water cooler pressured meal
the longing for the lonely dark
the lonely driving through the hills
the rock and roll the news the sports
the somnolence of lower speeds
the solitary cigarettes
and here upon a brazen hill
narcotic with the speed of light

I watch the always going home
the going west into the night . . .
—Gerald Locklin, "Long Beach Freeway"

Stereotypes to the contrary, most people who live in the tropic Southland do indeed go to work and earn their livings like everyone else. They do so in a region clouded by myth. It is now a desert-turned-metropolis, largely as a result of water piped from elsewhere—a classic western American pattern. Few today would suspect that the area south of the Tehachapi Mountains was called "the cow counties" even late in the nineteenth century, and was little touched by the Gold Rush; it remained largely Spanish-speaking through the 1860s. It also harbored a strong movement to split the state to avoid dominance by the economically and culturally advanced north. "At that time," writer Lawrence Clark Powell observes, "Los Angeles was the toughest town in the West, a cesspool of frontier scum."

While not a literary enclave like San Francisco, the region did produce an interesting body of writing in the nineteenth century. Most intriguing are Richard Henry Dana's early glimpses of Spanish California in *Two Years before the Mast*, a book that views the area as the first American settlers did, from the sea; William Manley's *Death Valley in '49*, which describes a tortuous overland approach; and a view of Los Angeles life in the 1850s, *The Reminiscences of a Ranger*, by Horace Bell, who was described by a contemporary as "blackmailer, murderer, thief, house-burner, snake-hunter, and defamer of the dead."

The pivotal work in Southern California's literary history is, of course, Helen Hunt Jackson's *Ramona*, published in 1884. Intended to expose the plight of Mission Indians, the book ironically became the major factor in the creation of a romanticized mission past. Judging by the number of people who today claim to *know* that the Ramona story is true, this appears to be an instance of myth filling a historical vacuum, sucked into reality by promoters.

Before long Southern California hosted a considerable middle-class, Middle-Western, White, Protestant society— complete with annual Iowa Picnics. One reason the place seems bizarre is that its nonconformists stand in high relief in such a social setting. But that seemingly conventional society has by no means been barren; early in this century it produced, for example, what Kevin Starr has aptly labeled the "literary Pasadenans"—Powell, M. F. K. Fisher, Hildergarde Flanner, Ward Ritchie—and even nourished the young Robinson Jeffers, a remarkable fluorescence indeed.

In the 1930s, a unique literary response to a changing world emerged here; crime and detective novels became a major mode of examining the effects of urbanization, industrialization, and frustration. James M. Cain, Raymond Chandler, and Ross Macdonald produced novels significant enough to force serious critical attention as well as a new sense of the price exacted by obdurate urban reality. As Chandler himself explained, his stories were set in "a world gone wrong where the law was something to manipulate for profit and power."

Today, the Southland is a cultural hodgepodge—wild, woolly, unpredictable, and exciting. It's fitting, then, that Charles Bukowski is probably the region's best-known contemporary writer. But there are plenty of others: Locklin, Ron Koertge, Wanda Coleman, Hisaye Yamamoto, Kate Braverman, Rafael Zepeda, Mitsyue Yamada, Frank Chin, and Alurista, among many others—another varied collection, most of whom wouldn't be caught dead in the waterfront dives favored by Bukowski. They might, however, be *found* dead in them.

In the midst of negative clichés and justifiable complaints about overpopulation, trendiness, and environmental problems, it is easy for other Californians to forget that SoCal is one of the world's most exciting cultural centers—it doesn't follow trends, it sets them. This region's air quality may be poor, but the caliber and variety of art in the greater L.A. area are high indeed.

The Southland's boundary with Fantasy California is Hollywood, that land of dreams. As Franklin Walker points out, although the 2,000-plus novels about the movie industry vary greatly, "nearly all agree that the life in the movie colony is artificial, the art meretricious, and the industry the graveyard of talent." Few have complained about the money, however.

Fantasy California

> *Cali-for-ni-ay!*
> *. . . The climate is better*
> *The ocean is wetter*
> *The mountains are higher*
> *The deserts are drier*
> *The hills have more splendor*
> *The girls have more gender*
> *—"Ca-li-for-ni-ay!"*

Spanish settlement of California began in the 1530s when a few brave souls ventured onto its southern reaches. Nothing those adventurers experienced, however, lived up to the image of the *name*, California, that had already been created in 1510 by Garci Rodriguez Ordonez de Montalvo in a popular Spanish novel, *Las sergas de Esplandian:* "There is an island called California, on the right hand of the Indies, very near the Earthly Paradise . . . inhabited by black women without a single man among them and living in the manner of Amazons. . . . Their arms are all of gold, as is the harness of the wild beasts which, after taming, they ride."

Welcome to Fantasy California. Not even Venice Beach or Telegraph Avenue has lived up to the expectations that followed, and disappointment has been common, especially in the responses of outsiders and newcomers. Even those who find what they expect may want more, or less, or something different. Observes writer Julian Marias, "Certainly, California is paradise. . . . [but] the excellences of Paradise are in the long run deficiencies in the 'real world.'" But Marias's "Paradise" is difficult to see for a cotton picker near Corcoran or a logger in Scotia or an oil worker at Maricopa—those places look very much like the "real world." Marias is writing about Fantasy California.

Another transplant, novelist Herbert Gold, explains in *Notes Towards an Understanding of California*:

> Elsewhere, there is struggle for existence; we have heard of this in California. Here, for the massive middle class, the struggle sometimes comes down to a courageous battle against boredom and bland, and this is why love and marriage seem to have replaced the frontier for exploration; they have become the moral equivalent of war in a state where all the marriages end in divorce.

Gold's observations are typical of the exaggeration this state stimulates, but tell that cotton picker, that logger, that oil worker, or perhaps a struggling Hmong family in a crowded Fresno apartment that "boredom and bland" are their toughest problems. No, with this generalization, Herb Gold too has tumbled into Fantasy California because he is using a caricature of the state to discuss a modern malaise.

For many, Fantasy California seems to be the *only* one, a

land of sun-bleached blondes with straight teeth, hurrying on roller skates to hot tubs after working in their marijuana fields or, in the last century, a place where gold nuggets could be scooped up by the shovelful and fruit burgeoned year-round. Unrealistic expectation leads to disillusionment: A homeless man at a San Francisco shelter said last Thanksgiving, "I thought California was about somethin', but it ain't about nothin'." This realm may not be a real place, but it certainly is a real idea or collection of ideas.

Fantasy California has, in any case, produced an intriguing body of literature in all of the physical regions. To this richly imaginative area can be assigned books as diverse as Evelyn Waugh's *The Loved One* (set in the Southland), Ernest Callenbach's *Ecotopia* (Wilderness California), Robert Roper's *Royo County* (Heartland) and Cyra McFadden's *The Serial* (Bay Area).

This fanciful realm even features two strangely similar yet diametrically opposed novels: Callenbach's aforementioned *Ecotopia*, which introduces a new nation embodying many "progressive" ecological dreams of the 1960s, and William Pierce's *Turner Diaries*, a neo-fascist, racist adventure about a group that captures much of California and creates a nation for whites only. Both are fantasies and both employ fictional Californias as their settings.

The apotheosis of Fantasy California's literature, however, is Nathaniel West's *The Day of the Locust*, published in 1939. As Powell explains, West wrote the novel "to formalize a tragic view of life. He perceived Hollywood and its product as the pure epitome of all that is wrong with life in the United States." *The Day of the Locust* is not a book about a real California; it is a book about Nathaniel West's response to a world gone mad. A hint of his attitude may be gleaned from a letter he wrote to Josephine Herbst in 1933 shortly after he had become a screenwriter: "This place is Asbury Park, New Jersey. . . . In other words, phooey on Cal. Another thing, this stuff about easy work is all wrong. My hours are from ten in the morning to six at night with a full day on Saturdays. There's no fooling here."

In any case, he produced a novel that typifies Fantasy Cal, a dark mirror limning the gap between expectation and reality. It is the area's greatest work because it combines those very elements with West's unique talent and sensitivity, extrapolating to national and international dimensions, toward a powerful surreal vision, all in the guise of a California. As West and others demonstrate, artists can find in the Golden State's complexity vehicles for writing about virtually anything—real or imagined.

An Actual California

There is an actual California—there are many of them, in fact, and they are both varied and unique. This remains a seeker's state, so it invites redefinition of the spirit's quest for the possible. Many non-natives come here and write; some even try to write about California. It is informative that in the best work produced here, no matter who writes it, the topography of the land is rarely far from the topography of the soul.

Let me try to illustrate what I mean by quoting from my own recent essay "The Kern, My River":

> In one sense, Kern River now stands as a symbol for all of California's once-wild streams: harnessed, directed, and utilized but not fully tamed. It retains an edge of wildness—the capacity for an occasional flash flood and more than an occasional drowning.

Human history is tied to it and human intervention has in places changed it beyond recognition. This river has, for instance, contributed mightily to the San Joaquin Valley's agricultural richness, depositing over the millennia thousands of acres of rich alluvial soil; now it irrigates many of those same acres.

To me, however, raised on its banks, it was simply "the river," the southern boundary of my parched hometown. A riparian forest lined the stream and, beyond that greenery, horned toads and jackrabbits and ants rested in the thin shade of tumbleweeds, while summer heat bent light into wet-looking waves. But always, as certain as sky and breath, those huge cottonwoods, those willows, those mysterious hanging vines, always those currents of chilled, crystalline water: Like most kids raised in Oildale, my life braided with the Kern, entwined with an intimacy that now seems extraordinary. I swam in its dangerous and forbidden waters, fished its pools and runs, explored on its wooded banks, attended the funerals of two friends who drowned in it. I ate food irrigated by it, drank its water, and stood mourning when its forest died and its bed became a sandy desert. I called it "the river," but thought of it as *mine*, my river.

Everything happens to particular people in particular places at particular times, so when we natives write, we call our settings California but really think of our personal Californias, because those places are real. They created us and we have created inner visions of them: the topography of our landscapes informing the topography of our soulscapes. As William Everson so eloquently sings of his California,

> *I in the vineyard, in green-time and dead-time, come*
>   *to it dearly*
> *And take nature neither freaked nor amazing,*

70

But the secret shining, the soft indeterminate
wonder.
I watch it morning and noon, the unutterable
*   sundowns,*
and love as the leaf does the bough.
                                —"San Joaquin"

Other Voices . . .
Other Lives

I N THE beginning there were native voices—Yokuts, Mojave, Hoopa, Miwok, Pomo—and they were eloquent, as this Yokuts death song illustrates:

> *All my life*
> *I have been seeking*
> *Seeking.*

Next came visitors like Mark Twain, Bret Harte, John Muir, William Henry Brewer, Ambrose Bierce, and Mary Austin. Today, California again produces its own authors, produces them in abundance, and the Great Central Valley, that vast, flat patchwork of fields and orchards in the center of California, the one that yields mountains of cotton, tons of raisins, oceans of jug wine, is also producing what seems an unlikely crop: more and better native writers than any other section of the state.

A list of prominent contemporary authors raised in this agricultural heartland would include, among many others, Maxine Hong Kingston (Stockton), Luis Valdez (Delano), William Everson (Selma), Joan Didion (Sacramento), Frank Bidart (Bakersfield), Leonard Gardner (Stockton), Gary Soto (Fresno), Robert Duncan (Bakersfield), Larry Levis (Selma), Sherley Anne Williams (Fresno), and Richard Rodriguez (Sacramento).

Significant writers from Stockton? From Fresno? From *Bakersfield?* You bet, and more are emerging all the time. They are creating a uniquely Californian literature, one that is rooted in a sense of place and is aware of the state's stereotype, one that is multiethnic and class conscious, one that is passionate and deeply concerned with the fecund but indifferent earth that makes Valley life possible. Most of all, it is a literature that refuses to hide the travail often necessary to achieve any measure of the California dream. Much Valley writing, like much Valley life, is hard-edged.

Williams, for example, explains, "My parents were migrant workers, following crops, and my father developed tuberculosis while we were in Fresno, so we stayed there." Her literature reflects that same frontal view; she opens "The Iconography of Childhood" this way:

73

Land flat as hoecake
Summers hot enough
to fry one crops fanned
out in fields far as
eyes can see
every
Time we work a row
another appears
on the horizon . . .

Writers blooded in this rugged realm seem, in the main, incapable of *not* writing about it. If some appear to abhor the place that was or is their home (Bidart, for instance), others seem to love it (Everson, for example). Most, however, project what might be called *involved ambivalence,* a tension that is revealed in the work of such authors as Soto, Didion, Gardner, and Hong Kingston. Involvement, not uncritical love, is the best index of a region's influence on its artists, and the Great Central Valley retains a profound clasp on artists raised here.

To comprehend why, one must first understand the Valley: some fifteen million acres, it is indeed "great." This region's apparently open and natural landscape is among the most dramatically altered nonurban settings in the world, with rivers dammed, native grasses replaced, indigenous wildlife despoiled, underground aquifers depleted; lately, even its naturally supine surface is being laser-leveled. The Valley is the apotheosis of agribusiness, industrial farming. There is yet another complication: every year thousands of this area's rich acres are being paved for urban and suburban development. It boasts the fastest-growing population in California.

All those things are reflected in the work of Valley authors, as are the wonders of the place: sudden glimpses of the Sierra Nevada after a rain, the olfactory delight of a summer evening, the ethereal dance of a dust devil dipping and swirling across the spring horizon, even the soft-focus intimacy of tule fog. William Everson, one of the region's first important native poets, writes in "Winter Sundown":

> *The fog, that nightlong and morning had lain to the*
> *   fields*
> *Earth-loving, lifted at noon, broke to no wind,*
> *Sheeted the sky blue-gray and deadened.*
> *The sun somewhere over the dark height ran steeply*
> *   down west;*
> *And that hour, silence hanging the wide and naked*
> *   vineyards,*
> *The fog fell slowly with twilight, masking the land.*

The area's other pioneering literary giant was William Saroyan. Like the Valley itself, he was unique, gifted, and difficult. In an essay entitled "Fresno" he observed the barren appeal of his hometown before it burgeoned into a city:

A man could walk four or five miles in any direction from the heart of our city and see our streets dwindle to land and weeds. In many places the land would be vineyard and orchard land, the weeds would be the strong dry weeds of the desert. In this land there would be living things that had their being in the quietness of deserts for centuries. There would be snakes and horned-toads, prairie-dogs and jack-rabbits. In the sky over this land would be buzzards and hawks, and the hot sun.

A younger artist, Bakersfield's Don Thompson, exemplifies the continued use of nature as correlate for a spiritual landscape in "On the Glennville Road,"

Oaks on the hillside,
like hoboes

in their ragged bark,
refuse to move on.

Stones slump to the ground,
exhausted . . .

Far to the north in Chico, Gary Thompson's "In the Wild Rice" accomplishes the same thing:

in the wild rice fields two rivers
meet;
one river from the north bears soil
so fertile that the dead
grow
in their graves.
the other carries the cleaned bones
and empty skin
of animals that once lived
inside the mountain snows. . . .

Still, the notion that these vast vacant fields, these vast vacant days might produce significant art defies comfortable assumptions. The land itself creates the impression: a promethean plain shimmering as though the soil is sweating; scattered towns paradoxically appearing dry as dice—what do people *do* here? This is certainly not the golden state of dreams, so few out-of-state artists have relocated in the Valley. Unlike coastal California, artists here tend to be homegrown.

Narrow geographic determinism does not explain the richness and complexity of art being produced in this vale; perhaps Richard Rodriguez's recollection of his hometown does:

"Sacramento nurtured me. . . . It became the scene of an extraordinary imagined life."

Real life can also be extraordinary in this area where parades and picnics remain major occasions, where fistfights still establish male territory, where some of the world's most creative agricultural technology continues to emerge.

Since many Valley writers leave the region for education or employment, enriched perspectives frequently render them unsanguine. They quickly recognize the ambivalent society that produced them, at once xenophobic and cordial, paternalistic and untrendy; saloons and churches define most communities and both are busy. The ironies of this dynamic, heterogeneous society rival nature as literary material for local artists.

Asked about her sense of the Valley, Sherley Anne Williams smiles and says, "I miss its southernness. It was settled by southerners, black and white, and it has many characteristics of the Old South, the conviviality, the limitations . . . as a black child, I was profoundly aware of what the society predestined me to do. Just lately I went back and talked to black youngsters who told me they had grown up being told not to go into the same towns that I'd heard not to go into."

She shakes her head. "But," she adds, "my son just started college at Chico State and it's comforting to know he's in the Valley. Isn't that strange?"

Ethnicity and class are tangled in this region that has attracted people willing to toil for some measure of success. Valley farming is truly agribusiness, the domain of vast corporations, and it has required legions of migrant laborers for seasonal employment. That fact has attracted the determined and the desperate—the Chinese and the Portuguese, the Slavs and the Japanese, the Armenians and the Basques: so many, so diverse—to what may be the most multiethnic rural area in the world, all of them willing to toil in these fields.

77

Fresno's geographic centrality symbolizes the state's racial richness in Lawson Fusao Inada's "California Heartland: The Exact Center":

> It doesn't matter to me
> that "the exact geographical center of California"
> is located in the back of the Gomez family yard.
> Or so they say . . .
> The Gomez family, the Inadas,
> are exactly where they are,
> where California starts from
> and goes out, and out, and out.
> From here, the going is easy.
> Look at our faces and smile.

It is particularly significant that those many cultures remain not merely memories hereabouts, but entities; cultural leveling is a slower process in this rural province. Los Baños poet Sam Pereira writes in "Dinner for Our Lady of":

> Banners from the old ways line
> The streets. Portugal takes
> California on Sunday. The easiest
> Day for it; the beaches full
> And the churches waiting.
> It's time for the statues
> To come out of hiding. Time
> For the saints to be carted down
> Blacktop 2 miles; up
> The steps to the hall, . . .

Sometimes those varied cultures clash and generational tension may rise, placing children—frequently already on their way to being more Californian than Filipino or Basque or Chinese—in the middle. In Hong Kingston's *The Woman Warrior* (1975), the author describes being sent to a Stockton drugstore with these orders from her unassimilated mother, who suspects that the druggist has placed a curse on the family:

> "You get reparation candy," she said. "You say, 'You have tainted my house with sick medicine and must remove the curse with sweetness.' He'll understand."
> "He didn't do it on purpose. And no, he won't, Mother. They don't understand stuff like that. I won't be able to say it right. He'll call us beggars."
> "You just translate." She searched me to make sure I wasn't hiding any money. I was sneaky and bad enough to buy the candy and come back pretending it was a free gift.

Paternalism bordering on a plantation mentality also developed locally. Social classes are poorly hidden in agricultural towns, and they profoundly influence the literature produced here. At the top are nonresident rich, mostly corporate owners, and resident rich who also control vast tracts of land or related industries.

Within those two small, elite groups exist tensions not only between old families and new ("My own childhood was suffused with the conviction that we had long outlived our finest hour," writes Didion), but also a vague embarrassment about the region that produces their wealth ("a ranch of my family's," Didion tells us, "with a slight rise on it, perhaps a foot, was known for the hundred-some years which preceded this year as 'the hill ranch.'")

For a long time Central Valley communities, like underdeveloped nations, boasted a relatively small middle class with few avenues entering it. Merchants and professionals and some family farmers were suspended between the tiny, powerful elite and the numerous marginal-to-poor people who constituted the backbone of the area's economy. The bourgeoisie tends to be scorned by intellectuals here as elsewhere. In *Golden State*, writes Frank Bidart:

> *The brown house*
> *on the brown hill*
> *reminds me of my parents.*
> *Its memory is of poverty,*
> *not merely poverty of means,*
> *but poverty of history, of awareness of*
> *the ways men have found to live.*

Like writing itself, such criticism is a luxury rarely open to the poor. It is immeasurably easier to indict deficiencies, and even to romanticize poverty, when you have not personally breathed its foul breath.

Destitution is rarely romantic, and in "Fog" Gary Soto—one of the many exceptional poets who developed at California State University, Fresno—exposes the absence of dignity bordering on despair that want may impose.

> *In Fresno, the fog is passing*
> *The young thief prying a windowscreen,*
> *Greying my hair that falls*
> *And goes unfound, my fingerprints*
> *slowly growing a fur of dust—*
> *One hundred years from now*
> *There should be no reason to believe*
> *I lived.*

When you're trapped in poverty, even that brown house on the brown hill may look like the promised land.

Fresno State, as the university is known, is surrounded by many brown houses, by many green fields, and it has become a remarkable center of poetic achievement in the past two decades. What's more—and more ironic—many poets trained at Fresno State now teach at universities that would not have admitted them as students.

Although some critics have asserted that Buck Owens and Merle Haggard best represent local literary taste, this San Joaquin Valley metropolis has produced—in writers such as Soto, Williams, David St. John, Luis Omar Salinas, Herbert Scott, Lawson Inada, Roberta Spear, Greg Pape, DeWayne Rail, Leonard Adame, Kathy Fagan, and Larry Levis, and others—a crop more unexpected than kiwi fruit or pistachios and far richer.

In retrospect, it seems that this valley was ripe for literary exploration by the time higher education became widely available following World War II. Fresno State was the hub when the area began to flower in the late 1950s, and local poets credit four teachers—Philip Levine, Peter Everwine, Robert Mezey, and C. G. Hanzlicek—with having encouraged and shaped their work. Levine, in particular, has offered an important model, and his arrival at Fresno in 1957 seems a remarkable example of fate: the right man reaching the right place.

The work of what are now proudly called the Fresno Poets increasingly graces the most prestigious collections of American verse. Asked how they account for this creative explosion, the writers themselves point toward Levine. "Phil was *enormously* encouraging to me," acknowledges Williams. "All I know," recalls Rail, "is that a whole world of possibilities opened up when I was at State studying with Phil. He was tough, but always honest." Thirty years ago Levine was hired by Fresno State College, a school that boasted no particularly literary reputation and no creative writing program at all.

81

Although he acknowledges that Fresno's literary emergence "had something to do with my being here and doing a decent job," Levine credits that special quality of his pupils: "I've never had a student at Fresno weep in class. One now-very-famous one told me to go fuck myself, in exactly those words. . . . I do better with people who have a little dirt in their teeth."

Part of the nineteen-campus California State University— what some have called the state's "blue-collar education system"—FSC was a solid school but hardly among America's educational elite, which probably made it just the right field for this unforeseen crop. As Levine says, "Stanford didn't exist for my students, then or now. None of these kids had that kind of loot or those connections." Ironically, because of "these kids," the school's poetic reputation is today national, even international. Certainly no school anywhere can boast recent poetic accomplishments superior to what is now officially named California State University, Fresno.

Today, with Valley cities burgeoning and even serving as suburbs for coastal megalopolises, with universities thriving in Chico, Davis, Turlock, Stockton, Sacramento, and Bakersfield, as well as Fresno, and with the local economy diversifying, the middle class is growing rapidly and, not coincidentally, so is literary output. Many local writers are the progeny of poverty, and they reflect in print the travail that allowed them to escape destitution. There seems always to be a touch of wonder, a tug of guilt, in such work, but little self-pity.

Wilma Elizabeth McDaniel's parents were Okie migrants, and her verse continues to explore variations of southwestern experience. In "Expenses" she writes,

> *Early rain*
> *set them back*

82

so strawberries are
expensive this year
so is life
at ninety-seven
It costs old Delbert
so much pain
to sit up in bed
and hold the carton
of glistening fruit
and smile at his
daughter
He manages to say
they sure are nice
and uses every cent
of energy
in his wornout
wallet

McDaniel frequently writes about impoverished folks, and the lower class may be divided into two groups in the Valley: One is the upwardly mobile poor, most of whom have achieved permanent residences of some sort and who provide steady blue-collar labor while their children take advantage of education and opportunity. The other is composed of those who still follow crops; recent arrivals, mostly, or longtime residents who have never escaped that desperate cycle.

One irony of deep poverty is that it frequently leads to materialistic yearning; as an old Okie woman once said, "Thangs, thangs, thangs is all these younguns want." In the opening paragraph of his story "Christ Has Returned to Earth and Preaches Here Nightly," Leonard Gardner has captured the grave if futile pride that "thangs" can provide the poor:

83

From the small, flat, hot valley town of Tracy, California—split by a highway and surrounded by fields of sugar beets, alfalfa, and tomatoes—an enormous pink car one day departed by the eastern end without previously entering by the western end, this car being the property of a permanent resident, Ernest Grubb, nineteen, who was in turn the property of a finance company. Ernest's fingernails were rimmed in black and there were black specks embedded in the blemishes on his cheeks. Painted on the rear fenders of the car, though it was only a week out of the showroom, were the words VALENTINO RETURNS.

Class consciousness has been an inescapable aspect of growing up in this place where some friends summered at the country club while others toiled in packing sheds. Traditionally, each socioeconomic class here has been larger and less white than the one above it; as a result, many of the region's most powerful writers are nonwhite: Williams, Soto, Hong Kingston, Valdez, Inada, Salinas, Jose Montoya, Leonard Adame, Oscar Peñaranda, Arnold Rojas, and more.

In their subjects and images, such authors—like many of their white counterparts—reveal that the California dream may have an underbelly as vivid as a trout's, as well as attendant cultural richness. Luis Omar Salinas writes in "Aztec Angel":

> . . . *I am the Aztec Angel*
> *Who frequents bars*
> *spends evenings*
> *with literary circles*
> *and socializes*
> *with spiks*
> *niggers and wops*
> *and collapses on his way*
> *to funerals . . .*

In 1863, William Henry Brewer led a geological survey party through the Great Central Valley. While nature here impressed him, the quality of society he found did not. On May 5 of that year he wrote, "I question if the next generation here will care for Shakespeare, or any other author, growing up in ignorance, far from school, church, or other institution of civilization." Others have been asking snide variations of that question ever since. It took time, of course—not until the emergence of Saroyan and Everson in the 1930s could high-quality writers be said to have developed locally, unless one claims Illinois-born Mary Austin—but now literature is a major product.

Why? Clearly, there has always been life aplenty to write about in the Valley: aspiration and conflict, disappointment and triumph. Frank Norris, Carey McWilliams, and John Steinbeck, among others, recognized that and employed this area as the setting for significant books. Robert Roper even set *Royo County*, an "anti-California" novel, here—acceptance, via negativa.

There is no "school" of writing from the Great Central Valley, although it seems that critics frequently label someone the "new Steinbeck," confusing both valleys and writers. In fact, variety and a certain toughness are the region's trademarks. Some artists remain here while others leave and look back; many deal with local vagaries of wealth and poverty in their work, with realms of hope and passion; some build their art on and of the soil, while others explore the cities. What most links them is their involvement with the harsh Valley that shaped them. Unexpected complexity dwells in this region; as Bakersfield's Phillip Feldman explains in "The Great Valley":

> *Like some books*
> *the Valley opens subtly.*
> *Its leaves turn slowly. . . .*

Most revealing is that many artists, like Riverdale's Art Cuelho, who now resides in Montana, find they cannot leave the Valley no matter where they go; he wrote in "The Harvest of Wheatville Longing":

> *I am planted here:*
> *my first kiss came*
> *from this land;*
> *lips of a sagebrush disk*
> *opened this adobe ground.*
> *My last longing harvest*
> *will be found here.*

It remains their heartland.

The Grapes of Wrath:
A Book That
Stretched My Soul

W E ALL went barefooted in 1952, so I literally hot-
footed it over scorching sidewalk up Chester Avenue to the Oildale branch of the Kern County Library, a small,
tree-shaded building that stood like an oasis in my desiccated
hometown. Fifteen years old, I had seen the movie version of
The Grapes of Wrath, hurried to the library, and searched the
fiction stacks for a copy of the novel. Not finding one, I asked a
librarian for help. She eyed me for an uncomfortable moment,
then asked, "What do you want with *that* book?"

"I was planning to read it," I stammered. She was a slim, stern woman who we kids suspected wore a wig, so we were certain she was baldheaded. Behind her back we referred to her as "Chrome dome."

"Yes," she snapped, "I suppose *you* were," her voice rich with implications. We stood for what seemed a long time and I shifted my weight from foot to foot. Then she added, "You'll need a note from your parents to check out that book."

"Okay," I replied, relieved. That would be easy.

"We keep *those* books here," she added, dipping her chin.

That explained it. Every kid in Oildale had heard that a cache of dirty books was stored within that high checkout desk near the door.

The Grapes of Wrath was published to wide critical acclaim on April 14, 1939. By the end of the month, Viking Press was shipping 2,500 copies a day; the number would grow to 10,000 in the summer when it was the nation's best-seller. It won both the National Book Award and the Pulitzer Prize and, of course, John Steinbeck was in 1962 awarded a Nobel Prize. Over 14,000,000 copies have now been sold, according to the Steinbeck Research Center at San Jose State University, including translations in at least twenty-six languages.

As far as I know, it did not win any awards in Kern County, and denunciations of the novel, as Steinbeck biographer Jackson Benson points out, "would come from editorials, and from the podium and pulpit." They sure would. W. A. Camp, then president of the Associated Farmers of Kern County, asserted, "we were attacked by a book obscene in the extreme sense." Given the xenophobia of the time and place, anything that didn't actively praise Kern County was apt to be judged offensive, and *The Grapes of Wrath* spent few words extolling the region. In my hometown, as in the rest of California, opponents scored the novel not only for its "obscenity" but for its asserted lack of truth and for its "communistic" slant.

The novel had been banned from the fall of 1939 until early 1941 by Kern County's Board of Supervisors, who pointed out that "John Steinbeck chose to ignore the education, recreation, hospitalization, welfare and relief services made available by Kern County." The ban caused the offending volume to be removed from the shelves of public and school libraries, but the book continued to be sold in local stores. While more self-serving than most, local supervisors were by no means unique in interpreting Steinbeck's novel only as social realism, and flawed social realism at that.

Purposely misreading the story was a common ploy and a publication of the Associated Farmers complained that Okie migrants "most certainly . . . are not the degenerate group that Steinbeck presented in his pleas for sympathy for them." In a pamphlet published by the same group, J. T. Miron asserted, "I can think of no other novel which advances the idea of class war and promotes hatred of class against class . . . than does *The Grapes of Wrath*." On the floor of the House, Congressman Alfred J. Elliot (D.-Tulare) perhaps summarized opposition when he declared, "It is the most damnable book that was ever permitted to be printed."

As it turned out, Kern County was already the scene of an anti-Okie movement when Steinbeck's novel was published. As the hub of the migration, Kern had severely strained public services—especially health and education. Resentment grew and many local citizens, themselves in tough economic binds, felt besieged. While unthinking dislike of the migrants was common, more than a few focused their animosity on the labor system of corporate agribusiness, which required a large work force of mobile poor. It slowly became clear that big agribusiness was benefiting at the expense of migrants and burghers alike.

In the rest of the state, and the rest of the country for that matter, most people either were unaware of the continuing stream of desperate Okies or simply ignored them. Great floods that began to inundate the Central Valley in January of 1938, however, at last threw the plight of struggling Okies into high relief. Reporters flocked to the swamped ditchbank communities and Hoovervilles; newspaper coverage forced this state's general public to recognize the migrants' plight. What resulted was a great outpouring of compassion and help from many.

A more ominous response, however, emerged because the sweetheart relationship between agribusiness and rural communities—some of which were virtually company towns—had begun to break down. A February 23, 1938, editorial in the *Bakersfield Californian* pointed out: "Every Californian must be concerned over a situation which creates an army of migrant laborers who are left without employment. . . . it would appear that if the grower is directly advantaged, indirectly he and all the other permanent residents of the state are disadvantaged."

Kern County high rollers—including Alfred Harrell, publisher of the *Californian*—sensing that the economic status quo was in jeopardy, formed the Committee of Sixty to deal with the "peril to every working man and woman . . . in the migrant labor and relief problem of Kern County." Steinbeck's novel had dramatically increased national interest in the plight of the migrants so, as Walter Stein explains in *California and the Dust Bowl Migration*, "with public interest focused on the Okies, growers' organizations coalesced with the state's economy bloc to launch a major campaign against the migrants." The Committee of Sixty soon evolved into the ultraconservative statewide California Citizens Association.

By the time I entered the Oildale library thirteen years later, the fuss had largely died down, but the novel was still un-officially taboo. Even in my house, as it turned out. To my astonishment, my parents refused to write a note for me. That was a first. When I asked why, my mother simply said, "It's a filthy book and I won't have you reading it."

Since I had already read—or read selected underlined pas-sages of—certain minor classics that passed from teenage boy to teenage boy in those days, that dual refusal guaranteed that I'd peruse *The Grapes of Wrath* as soon as possible.

I was working weekends then on a farm, so I had money of my own. After school Friday, I rode a city bus four miles into Bakersfield, where I purchased for twenty-five cents a paper-back copy of the novel. I carried it to the fields with me when I went to work early Saturday morning and was able to com-plete the forbidden novel during spare time that weekend while irrigating on a spread between Arvin and Edison.

It turned out not to be the erotic tale I had anticipated, but I wasn't disappointed. Its message about the human spirit hit me where I lived. The great, the ennobling theme of Steinbeck's work—we are a human family, together in this, and collec-tively we can transcend life's challenges—reached into me and stretched my soul. I was enthralled.

At fifteen I was titillated by the mere word "breast." None-theless, the novel's controversial final scene in which Rose of Sharon suckled a starving man seemed so appropriate, so reli-gious, that it was not sexually provocative. It was, in fact, a little frightening because I sensed that it was dealing with something portentous.

More to the point, unlike *Silas Marner*, *The House of Seven Gables*, and the other books I was required to read in high school, *The Grapes of Wrath* dealt with people and places I recognized. A couple of miles from the ranch where I worked, on the rise above Caliente Creek, was the spot where the

Joads had first sighted the Valley, where Pa Joad declared, "I never knowed they was anything like her." Ruthie and Winfield would have been about my age; I might have dated her, played ball against him. For the first time in my life I had encountered significant literature about something real.

But there was more. Although I then dwelled in a class-conscious society among Joads and their relatives, although I had chopped cotton with families that still lived in broken-down cars, although I had more than once accompanied my own father on picket lines and had heard us referred to as "Oil-dale Okies," the book conveyed absolutely no social message to me at the time.

Perhaps it was because I was in the midst of it, so no perspective presented itself. There were poor folks who didn't get enough money, rich folks who didn't get enough sex, and folks in the middle who didn't get enough of either: so what? I didn't yet understand corporate agribusiness or peonage or exploitation; I didn't realize that the San Joaquin Valley was already the richest farming area in the world or how important a poor, malleable, mobile work force was to that reality. All those things I learned only much later. As a result, I seemed to read past the very material that had so outraged the Associated Farmers, the Committee of Sixty, the California Citizens Association, and the state chamber of commerce, among others.

I asked several neighbors—themselves ex-migrants—about the novel and can recall that Mrs. Pruett, who lived next door, snapped something like "That Steinbeck"—the name hissed with deep scorn—"and his nasty words! Decent folks don't talk thataway." Mr. Clay's eyes flared, and he said something that I can paraphrase as, "That sumbitch oughta mind his own damn business." Buford Roy Daniels, one of my fellow irrigators, had an unambiguous opinion: "That Steinbeck guy's full of it."

None had read the book, and neither had anyone else I talked to in Oildale or on the ranch where I worked.

No one I asked had anything good to say about the novel or its author, but no one ever mentioned agricultural economics or unions or sedition either. I heard those things three years later, along with considerable praise for *The Grapes of Wrath*, when I was a student at Bakersfield Junior College. No, everyone I queried in 1952 alluded to foul language, to nasty scenes, to demeaning characterizations. Even a lady I met who taught in the elementary school at Edison, and who had actually read the book, said, "It was well-intended, I'm sure, but *so* raw."

I seemed to have read a different novel. The characters in *The Grapes of Wrath* talked just like Buford Roy Daniels, like Mr. Clay and Mrs. Pruett, like the Bundys, the Haggards, the Purvises and the Hillises with whom we lived and socialized. But Steinbeck's Joads were an economic notch below those good people, in part because our Oildale and Arvin friends had already begun to make it in the Golden State by the time I knew them: They were working, they were buying houses, their kids were attending school. Earlier hardships remained unrevealed because they did not seek pity.

But scars remained, and the word "Okie," used injudiciously, could lead to mayhem. While the term could be traced as far back as 1905, Ben Riddick of the *Los Angeles Times* popularized its use during the migration. Eventually it became a generalized pejorative in California. Sometimes its use was amusing: Oildale guys called farm kids Okies while they, in turn, were called the same thing by their Bakersfield neighbors who, of course, were often termed Okies by big-city cousins in L.A. It meant country, it meant bumpkin, it meant someone we're better than, and it could cost you your teeth if you weren't careful. More than a few migrants actually blamed Steinbeck for having popularized both the word and the stereotype, but that was nonsense.

Not until the summer after I read the novel did I encounter someone who would talk about its social reality and local impact. Jimmy Fix was my father's age, a member of the Democratic Central Committee and a dedicated union man. He was from an old Bakersfield family, and he dripped disdain for the town's power structure. "As long as those knotheads could exploit the Okies without any trouble for themselves, they did. Once people caught on and gave those big money boys some hell, though, the big shots pretended they were patriots saving the state, and the [Bakersfield] *Californian* was right in the big middle of it. They did everything they could to make things rough on those poor people.

"But there were a lot of good folks around here—teachers, doctors, just plain working folks—who were trying to help. They didn't have the connections or the money those high powers did, but at least they were trying to do the right thing. When Steinbeck's book was published, the *Californian* did everything in the world it could to attack it, but there was a code: you avoided social or economic threats because those were areas you didn't want discussed at all except on your own terms, so if you *did* talk about them you damn sure didn't mention big agribusiness, you talked about a threat to small farms, to the American Way of Life, to people's daughters, crap like that, and you equated any dissent with communism.

"Naw, the plan was to convince people who *hadn't* read the book, and probably *wouldn't*, that it was dirty, morally corrupt, to let them become unofficial censors."

Despite such revelations, my first magical reading of the novel had convinced me that its greatest power was not social and political but mythic and spiritual. The social and political references are for me a bonus and a compelling dimension, but

94

they have never seemed primary. The book does not pretend to be an accurate history of the Okie migration, but it is indeed an accurate evocation of the human spirit's resiliency. Steinbeck's art exceeded documentation, so you must go to his book for truth, not facts.

Thirty-five years after initially reading Steinbeck's great novel I was speaking to a friend named Clyde Nance who, with his parents, had migrated to California during the thirties. "We didn't look like *The Grapes of Wrath,*" he smiled, "no mattress on the car, but we were sure glad to get to Salida outside Modesto. My father got a job driving in grape stakes for Gallo for fifteen cents an hour. A little later he got a better job at another farm, it paid two bits an hour. One month he brought home a hundred dollars.

"I tried to explain to my son what that means—*four hundred hours of work*—but I couldn't. It's all too different nowadays. They are and I guess I am. We're Californians. But I haven't forgotten."

"Steinbeck would understand," I said.

"You reckon?" he grinned.

"I reckon."

Father Comes Home

I AWAKEN IN dead darkness, suddenly alert. A clouded voice is calling, calling like a departing dream: "Gerry . . . I need you."

It is Pop.

I find him tangled in his bed, unable to free himself from a urine-soaked sheet. He does not at first seem to recognize me, his toothless mouth working, his eyes thick and dazed. Time hangs there, then he smiles and his voice quivers, "Get me outta here."

I do that, help him strip and clean himself, then dress once more. I make no issue of his problem for, despite the multi-infarct dementia that diminishes responses, he remains profoundly troubled by his incontinence. As I remake his bed, he shuffles into a nearby bathroom. When he returns, there is another dazed moment, followed by a smile. My father remembers me.

AND I REMEMBER HIM—young, wearing a white T-shirt freckled with petroleum from his job, smelling vaguely of beer. Home from a day in the Kern River oil fields, he was rummaging through our garage, a small disaster of wires, of pipes, of fixtures—the trappings of a part-time electrician, his second job. Having matured during the Great Depression, work was sacramental to him.

Occasionally, during those years, he'd wrestle with me, our only form of physical contact, for it was difficult for him to display affection. My mother's face was often troubled as she watched us romp. "Take it easy, Speck," she'd urge, "you'll get him all worked up." Rough stuff upset her and she always seemed fragile.

Today, despite her own health problems, she seems relatively resilient, residing semi-independently in a nearby mobile-home park. My father, living with us, is vulnerability itself, so stripped by brain damage that he can hide no emotion: tears and grins come without resistance to a face once carefully controlled.

Our present arrangement is a gentle paradox. Although I was raised in a household that included aging relatives, all were from Mom's family—Hispanic, intimate, and large. Great-grandma, Uncle Tudy, and Grandma lived with us during their final years and died with us. My father, who had himself left

97

home at thirteen and always seemed distant in family matters, was generous without being warm. "He was embarrassed by the way we loved one another," my mother tells me, "and jealous, so he talked rough, but he never turned anyone away." Perhaps that is why it has never occurred to me, an only child, that my folks *wouldn't* one day join us.

POP SOMETIMES TOOK ME to work with him at the Shell Oil tank farm north of Oildale where we lived, introducing me to his pals as "my tax exemption," an appellation I did not understand but liked because it was something special between us. After work, he would stop at a blue-collar beer bar, the Tejon Club, to sip suds with other working men, laugh, perhaps shoot snooker. He'd buy me a soft drink and allow me to sip the foam from his draft.

There was a mild irony in his satisfaction with that gang, because my father had attended UCLA and felt intense, festering dissatisfaction at not having graduated, at having been consigned to blue-collar work. He rarely talked about his college experience—not to me, at least. It was an experience turned so dark that it had to be buried, like the souvenirs of his All-America football career that he kept buried in a chest in his room.

He does not, however, bury his affection for the girl I married. Jan's very presence buoys him. Since he has lived with us, I am sensing the great breadth of her love as she cares for this sometimes difficult old man. In fact, Jan does more for Pop than I do, avoiding no chore, and performing each with grace and good humor.

I am also observing adolescent children put their rebellions aside to comfort Grandpa, then pick them up again to deal with us. A boy who drips teenaged condescension at Jan and me, curling his lip at us, prepares his grandfather's lunch, then patiently sits with the ailing man, helping him eat. He does this without pay, without coercion, without complaint.

This is true in part because Jan and I do the great bulk of work involving my dad, and distribute other tasks so that no individual is overburdened. But there is more: since Grandpa has joined us, we have seen elements of compassion, responsibility, and maturity not previously manifested in our children.

Last Friday, my wife and I took the night off and attended a concert. When we returned, Garth and Carlos, who had remained home, were both grinning. "Grandpa came out in his underpants and said, 'Tighten my belt,'" explained Garth. "We gave him some ice cream, then put him back to bed." His smile was genuine, his voice reflective.

Most of our friends have been strongly supportive, actually exaggerating the difficulty of our situation. A few, however, seem to consider our new familial arrangement an implicit indictment of their own. "We're taking care of *ourselves*," a friend volunteered with quivering chin not long ago. It was a cri de coeur, for I knew that her own desperately ill mother lived in a nursing home, something I had not mentioned and would not. No two situations are the same.

Such responses are understandable, though. Our society has increasingly faced dying and death, but progressive debilitation remains a wilderness. Several years ago, when it appeared that prostate cancer would kill my father, our family talked about death, its inevitability and consequences. We were prepared. Now a more ominous truth hovers before my children's eyes and ours: Grandpa's slow unraveling—that bright, tough man coming apart before our eyes.

Arthritis forced Pop to retire fifteen years ago when he was sixty-two. Today, although he retains the thick trunk that once carried efficient musculature, the muscles themselves are gone

—atrophied, ravaged, emptied. Moreover, he once moved with leonine grace and seemed capable of almost any physical feat. Yesterday, he shuffled uncertainly into the front yard—brain damage has destroyed his steps—and asked if he could help us. I handed him a rake and for a quarter-hour he carefully groomed a three-foot area until, in the manner of those suffering from locomotor ataxia, he worked his way into a position he could not change and gradually grew stiff as a statue. He did not request help, but raged—"You son of a bitch!"—at the body that has failed him. I eased him into a comfortable stance, thanked him, then asked if he'd like a cup of coffee.

DURING MY ADOLESCENCE, POP seemed determined not to encumber me with his reputation as an outstanding athlete. Nonetheless, I knew that I could never match it and I was right. Although I too played college football, I was not in his class. He had been one of the golden boys of autumn, a UCLA Bruin who, at only 165 pounds, had twice in the early 1930s been awarded Honorable Mention as a guard on the Walter Camp All-America Football Team. Typical of him, his certificates were never displayed but were secreted in his room. Mom showed them to me.

At the senior citizens meal he attends each weekday afternoon, Pop shuffles to his accustomed place, then sits silently awaiting service. I seat myself as usual in the back of the room. My father looks forward to this social contact—it is the high point of his day—although he speaks little when there.

He seems, moreover, not to notice the condescending behavior of some other seniors there, the smirks at the two inoperable wristwatches he insists on wearing, at his refusal to use his false teeth, at his hat which is frequently askew. Pop appears not to notice them, but I do, and I have inherited a degree of his pugnacity, so I steam silently and bite my tongue.

Today, however, a regular who has been disdainfully referring to my father as "Willie," despite knowing his given name, approaches me and asks, "Did your father play football?"

It seems a non sequitur and I eye him momentarily, then nod.

"He wasn't Speck Haslam, was he?" I nod once more. "Jeeze," he says, then he returns to his table and I hear him mumbling to others, "That guy was Speck Haslam, the football player."

I hear only the past tense, but the present tense most concerns me.

A couple of weeks after Pop moved in with us, we entertained two close friends. They are about the same age as my wife and I, and they have interrupted their careers and are now parents of their first child. Delighted, they have in the manner of other well-educated, affluent cronies attended seminars and workshops on parenting, among other topics.

As we sipped wine that afternoon, the new mother announced, "Well, we're finally understanding what you guys went through—the diapers, the sleepless nights . . ."

Jan and I exchanged smiles for we have slowly returned to patterns of early parenthood ("Guess what Pop said today . . .") and are bemused at our own behavior.

"Oh," she said, "that's right. You're sandwich generationers"—a term she had picked up at an expensive workshop. It is accurate because we truly are sandwiched between our five children and my failing parents, and it has so far been a revealing, demanding, and strangely satisfying experience.

LAST SUMMER WE TOOK Pop to a pioneer picnic in Santa Maria, his hometown. There a large, robust-looking man about my father's age approached us and extended his right hand. Pop

101

did the same, automatically but without recognition. When the
man tried to speak with him, my dad could not respond, his eyes
dull as clay. For a moment the man gazed into his face, then
he turned toward me, tears welling from his own eyes, and chal-
lenged, "I hope you know *who this guy was. I hope you know*
he was student body president. He was an All-American, for
Christ's sake. He stayed after practice to help the rest of us. I
hope you know. . . ." The man could not continue.

I could say nothing because, in truth, I *didn't* know exactly,
but I do see the sum of my father's life when I look at him, and
that is difficult for my children. Old age is difficult for them;
they tend to view it as a static state: Gramps was always old and
they've always been young. But slowly, certainly, as they too
attend pioneer picnics or read old press clippings or view old
photographs—*"That's* Grandpa? He was *cute"*—slowly, certainly, life's inexorability and death's inevitability become real.
We're in this together.

We are by no means martyrs. Our situation is eased by the
fact that we hire help five days a week, so our work schedules
have been little altered by Pop. And our kids have not only attended their grandfather but have also endured without protest
some dislocation; Carlos had to switch rooms so Pop could
be ensconced close to the master bedroom, and Simone has
moved in with her grandmother.

They do not protest, but they do study us. There are moments when I see one of them gazing from me to Grandpa and
back while I am helping my dad or, more significantly, when
I am fighting my own resentment at work delayed or intimacy
interrupted by him. My parents, my children, my wife, and I
are exploring some secret chambers. Our lives are deeply entwined and my mother, with more than a touch of irony, tells

my wife, "Gerry always wanted to be Speck's boy. Now he's got his wish."

Difficulties do not dominate our lives. We deal with what we must and my father's condition is a reality. Jan and I changed diapers for five youngsters, now we do it for my father—a task the kids, of course, are spared. An unspoken pattern has emerged in our lives. My wife and I try to cover for one another, to make certain neither of us is constantly on duty. If Jan re-made Pop's bed in the morning, I make certain to do it in the afternoon. If she walked him yesterday, I'll walk him today. And we try to allow our behavior toward Pop—*how* we do things—to speak our feelings.

If this family's experience is at all typical, it may suggest that, as a society, we are losing a vital aspect of human relationships if we don't see lives through to their conclusions. There are vital lessons being learned in our house now and no one is lecturing.

Pop shuffles into the living room; this is one of his bad days, one of his addled ones, and he is trying to pull red pajama bottoms on over his trousers. "Dad," Alexandra asks with sudden gravity, "will that happen to you?"

"It could, hon'," I reply, not telling her that she has touched my great fear. "It could happen to any of us."

Grandpa sometimes gets the children confused: Alexandra is Simone, Garth is Carlos, Fred is me. But he consistently grins in their presence, seeming to thrive on the action around our house. Our dogs and cats are special delights to him. His grandchildren introduce him to their friends with no apparent embarrassment. At times, they can't help grinning at my father's antics—the sort of things he once found so funny in aging in-laws—when, for example, he stands behind my chair and loosens his belt, then pokes my shoulder and demands,

"Aren't you gonna tighten me?" At other times, though, that same caper leaves them pensive.

Life is full of cycles and circles. I was a bed wetter as a child and my father had been embarrassed. "We can't take him *anywhere*," he told my mother when I was seven or eight years old, looking away from me as he spoke. I plotted vengeance then for the humiliation I attributed to him. Well, now's my chance, but all I want to do is to take care of him, make what's left of his life as pleasant as it can be, and I have allies in that quest.

LAST NIGHT WHEN I tucked Pop into bed, I gave his feet a sharp tug before I said goodnight, and he giggled.

Welcome home, Pop.

What about the Okies?

T HE PROGENY of the Okies—those poor, tough, often desperate, always hopeful people who clawed their way west during the Depression—have matured and stabilized; today they have assumed a fair share of economic and political power in California, especially in the Great Central Valley. But their position was not always so comfortable. In 1939 a sign posted at the entrance of a Bakersfield movie theater summed up their situation: "Niggers and Okies upstairs."

105

That sign symbolized the Okies' ambiguous position in California's class- and race-conscious agricultural regions during the 1930s. "Lord," recalls one woman who lived through it, "that was a hard time."

Who were the Okies and where did they come from? While Oklahoma was the focus of attention, the actual migrants drifted in from across the Great Plains, north and south: the Dakotas, Nebraska, Kansas, Missouri, Texas, Arkansas, and Oklahoma, especially the last four. At Edison, just outside Bakersfield, in April 1938, Paul Schuster Taylor found 150 families in a squatters' camp near potato sheds. Their auto licenses were from Minnesota, Missouri, Oklahoma, Arizona, California, Texas, Nebraska, Mississippi, Utah, New Mexico, Oregon, and Washington.

Still, they were all "Okies" once they reached the Central Valley. The word itself has been traced back to 1905, but its use in the 1930s as a generally derogatory term for any white migrant stuck. Today, in the Valley a siphon hose used for stealing gas is an "Okie credit card"; Arizona cattlemen call their poorest stock "Okies." During the late 1960s Dewey Bartlett, then governor of Oklahoma, tried to alter the word's connotation for the better by billing it as an acronym ("Oklahoma, Key to Intelligence and Enterprise"), but he had little luck.

Fittingly, the recent work of second-generation Okie migrants—especially but not exclusively Merle Haggard—has reintroduced pride in the term. Says Jim Young, chancellor of Bakersfield College, "I'm proud of my folks and everyone else who came out here and were called Okies, and who made new lives for themselves." Young, of course, symbolizes well why others in the Central Valley are so proud to claim that term, Okie. In fact—and to paraphrase the Joads, "who woulda thunk it"—what might be called "Okie Chic" developed in the Central Valley a few years ago: fake Okies—white folks who suddenly pulled on cowboy boots, affected drawls, and developed a love for the nasal deliveries of Hank Snow and Kitty Wells. In all likelihood this was a way of joining what many considered to be a minority group at a time when pluralism was in. Okies (the group was heterogeneous, the term an invention) constituted a unit that whites could temporarily join.

Nonetheless, some Oklahomans today remain resentful over its use to describe "Depression drifters." A judge from the Sooner State wrote to me some years ago to say that the migration to the coast had raised the IQ's of both states; I responded simply that I couldn't say what the move had done for Oklahoma, but that California was a better place because of it.

What forced the migrants from their native states to the West Coast? Surely it was dust, as Woody Guthrie so powerfully proclaimed. Although the Dust Bowl was certainly involved, it was a comparatively small area contrasted with the range of places from which migrants departed; explains Paul Bloomfield in *The Dust Bowl*, the region's core consisted of northwest Texas, northeast New Mexico, southeast Colorado, west Kansas, and the Oklahoma panhandle.

Many people who lived through the migration identify dust storms as the cause for their move. Understandably so, for the storms were visible and dramatic—at Guymon, Oklahoma, in March 1935, Vernon Hopson saw a full fifty-five-gallon oil drum fly by his window during a storm. One bit of folk humor was that to build a wind gauge, you should tie a logging chain to a big tree: if the chain stood straight out, it was breezy; if it whipped like an angry snake, there was some wind; if the tree and chain were gone, there had been significant wind; if you could see any of this, however, there was no dust worth mentioning. Guthrie was in Pampa, Texas, in April 1935 when a "black blizzard" struck and, uncertain whether he would survive the storm, he began writing "So Long, It's Been Good to

Know You." People don't easily forget those kinds of experiences.

Still, the most popular myth arising out of the 1935–40 migration was a tendency to overemphasize the importance of dust storms. "Dustbowler" remains one synonym for "Okie." In fact, much of middle America was on the move, and most Okies did not come from the Dust Bowl; there had actually been proportionately larger migrations from that region during earlier droughts.

The major causes of the migration, as traced by Walter Stein in *California and the Dust Bowl Migration* and documented in numerous studies, were the following:

1. Mechanization of farming
2. New Deal crop curtailment policies
3. Tenant farming practices
4. Drought
5. Soil depletion
6. Rural poverty
7. Economic Depression

Tractors—the hated "Farmalls"—symbolized the end for a great many marginal agricultural people, because mechanization allowed large farms to be operated more efficiently and thus less expensively. Closely related to the impact of mechanization were the changes caused by crop curtailments under the aegis of the Agricultural Adjustment Acts; the cotton crop was cut by a third, with subsidies paid to owners, not to tenants or seasonal laborers. In turn, this led to a major, probably inevitable economic upheaval, since many owners bought farm machinery with their subsidy payments, creating a cycle that forced large numbers of rural folk—not all farmers, by any means—to seek new vistas.

The drought that parched the Great Plains after 1931 was, of course, also a major factor in the Okie migration. That region had been subject to recurrent dry spells, as John Wesley Powell had predicted in 1878, and a boom-bust economy developed. Despite the allure of 160-acre homesteads, it became clear early that small farms in the region would be hard pressed to survive. When the busts came, many a Populist blamed "Eastern money interests" for his problems, but the drought cycle, as well as poor soil conservation on the part of farmers, were equally important. The plainsmen's dislike for Eastern banks was captured by Alastair Cooke:

> It was out on the prairie that the people felt most cheated and disheartened. They had gone out to realize the dream of free men and free soil . . . the homesteaders were now in hock to the money makers who had beguiled them into feeding two continents, and doing it too well.

A basic American dream, it seemed to farmers, was being destroyed, and "Eastern money interests" were indeed a long way from blameless.

The combination of high interest payments and escalating railroad freight rates, which made shipping produce from the Okie states to Eastern markets barely profitable, led to widespread rural poverty, affecting not only farmers but also all who depended upon them for a livelihood. When the Depression hit, large numbers could hold on no longer; as Stein points out, it was low farm income fostered principally by the other listed causes that finally supplied the impulse to move. John Steinbeck's view in *The Grapes of Wrath* was a simple, powerful mixture of fact and fiction:

> The squatting men looked down again. What do you want us to do? We can't take less share of the crop—we're half starved

now. The kids are hungry all the time. We got no clothes, torn an' ragged. If all the neighbors weren't the same, we'd be ashamed to go to meeting.

And at last the owner men came to the point. The tenant system won't work any more. One man on a tractor can take the place of twelve or fourteen families. Pay him a wage and take all the crop. We have to do it. We don't like to do it. But the monster's sick. Something's happening to the monster.

Capitalism was Steinbeck's monster. Finally, poor folks had to move.

Move they did, with over 500,000 people drifting west, usually along parallel lines, that is, migrants from the Northern Plains moved to the Pacific Northwest, while migrants from the Southern Plains tended to settle in Arizona and California. In all, something over 350,000 people finally migrated to California from the Okie states. Arizona, while absorbing far fewer migrants in actual numbers, acted as both a conduit for many of the California-bound and a long-term home for others. The famed country singer Buck Owens, for example, moved from Sherman, Texas, to Mesa, Arizona, where he was raised. Eventually he settled in Bakersfield, where he achieved prominence.

Arizona offered a natural haven for those Okies blooded in a cotton culture, since cotton was the state's main cash crop. Growers there were not naive; they saw clearly the possibility of cheap, experienced labor. The following advertisement appeared in the *Daily Oklahoman* on October 13, 1937:

Cotton Pickers. Several thousand still wanted to arrive here before November 15th; growers paying 5 cents short staple . . . houses or tents free; ideal climate . . . Farm Labor Service, 2 West Jefferson, Phoenix, Ariz.

The residence requirement for relief in Arizona was raised to three years in 1937, thus allowing growers to entice Okies to chop and pick Arizona cotton, which matured earlier than California's, then encourage migrants to move on when there was no more work locally. It was not unusual for people to follow ripening crops from Arizona to California's Imperial Valley, then north to the Great Central Valley, and sometimes even farther north and west to the Santa Clara and Salinas valleys. A *New York Times* reporter called it "the neatest get-rich-quick scheme of the century" because Arizona got the labor it needed but few of the attendant headaches.

"Two great social catastrophes, the Depression and World War II," Lawrence Clark Powell pointed out recently, "made Arizona what it is today." The first of these two included in no small measure the contribution made by desperate Okies, for while farm wages plunged, acreage under cultivation in the state actually increased. On the other hand, the large numbers of migrants—some transient, some permanent—considerably increased pressures on public services, especially schools and other arenas of social intercourse in Arizona, as in California. This was compounded by the fact that most Okies refused to passively accept second-class citizenship; they remained fiercely independent. Said one migrant, "We ain't no paupers. We hold ourselves to be white folks. We don't want no relief. But what we want is a chanst to make an honest living like what we was raised."

California, not Arizona, was the ultimate magnet for most migrants. Why? Single-cause explanations, such as the conservatives' claim that the Golden State's "overly liberal" welfare program lured Southwesterners, and the liberals' contention that growers seduced vast numbers with handbills, do not stand up to historical scrutiny. In fact, it now appears that proportionally more growers in Arizona than California employed handbills to attract workers; moreover, only in February when there was little or no field work did welfare rolls in agricultural regions of the state shoot up.

No ploy was necessary to attract migrants in any case: California was the nation's ultimate destination, the place where it never rained and everything burgeoned; Okies were no more immune to what Kevin Starr has called the California Dream than were other Americans. The constant boosting of the state in national media that had gone on since the Gold Rush was certainly an important factor, for a mystique had developed and poor people who had never visited California nonetheless created an inner vision of it. Wrote the Mississippi bard and singer Jimmie Rodgers in "California Blues": "I'm going to California / where they sleep out every night." Rodgers never set foot in the Golden State. As Frederick Jackson Turner early recognized, the West in general seemed a land of opportunity; it had become an American habit to drift west during hard times.

Researchers found two major factors cited by Okies for their migration: (1) The desire to join other, earlier migrants, usually relatives or friends, and (2) a belief that jobs were easier to find and paid better out West. What migrants found, finally, was often not what they had expected.

In fact, the coming of Okies catalyzed enduring California problems forced near the surface by the Depression. California agriculture was an industry concentrated in the Imperial, Sacramento, and San Joaquin valleys, although other areas were also productive. So diverse was the state's production that by 1930 some 180 different commercial crops were grown here.

One salient but unhappy fact for newcomers was that the state was not a place where small farmers might start again. It was, and remains, dominated by agribusiness. Further, the California system of agriculture has required large numbers of seasonal workers, and growers have traditionally found an abundant labor force, with attendant low wages, the rule. Historically, many field laborers were nonwhite: from the 1870s to the 1930s, for example, Chinese, Japanese, East Indians, Mexicans, and Filipinos had been major laboring groups, along with various whites "on the bum." Ironically, many Okies were Southerners in their racial attitudes, and some had left their native states rather than do "nigger work"; in California, many did anything they could, often accepting wages turned down by nonwhites.

Okies did create one especially troubling problem in agricultural communities, most of which were small and tightly knit: These migrants intended to settle down, not follow crops endlessly, and most were white, so they could not be as easily distinguished and isolated. Moreover, California's agricultural counties, for all their open space, could not easily absorb large numbers of newcomers, for their economic bases were narrow. Nonetheless, all the Okies seemed to be seeking somewhere to settle and take root, and they kept coming. Madera County's population grew by 35 percent between 1935 and 1940; Monterey County by 36 percent, San Diego County by 38 percent, Tulare by 38.4 percent, Kings by 38.5 percent, Yuba by 50.3 percent, and Kern, the hub of the migration, by a whopping 63.6 percent.

With small towns unable and often unwilling to absorb them, large numbers of Okies set up tents, lived out of cars, or built wood-and-cardboard hovels such as the ones photographed near Nipomo in 1936 by Dorthea Lange. The *San Francisco News* immediately contacted United Press and published the photos on March 10 under the headline "Ragged, Hungry, Broke, Harvest Workers Live in Squalor." United Press alerted relief authorities who, in turn, rushed food to the desperate migrants. Lange's documentary photographs rank with Steinbeck's writing as great artistic expressions of the time.

For most local residents, however, the Okie settlements were primarily embarrassments; everyone agreed that living conditions were horrible. Steinbeck powerfully described life in a so-called ditch-bank camp in his often-forgotten masterpiece of proletarian writing, *Their Blood Is Strong*. Wrote Steinbeck in part:

> The three-year-old child has a gunny sack tied about his middle for clothing. He has the swollen belly caused by malnutrition.
>
> He sits on the ground in the sun in front of the house, and the little black fruit flies buzz in circles and land on his closed eyes and crawl up his nose until he weakly brushes them away.
>
> They try to get at the mucous in the eye-corners. The child seems to have the reactions of a baby much younger. The first year he had a little milk, but he has had none since.
>
> He will die in a very short time. . . .

Tragically, a great many children did die, for the combination of exposure and poor diet made Okies especially vulnerable to diseases that the general populace usually avoided. Typhoid was common because of bad water; smallpox epidemics occurred in the San Joaquin and Imperial valleys; pneumonia, malaria, and tuberculosis, as well as internal parasites, took heavy tolls.

Fearing that pestilence would spread to towns, some county officials closed dirt-bank settlements, but such moves ultimately solved nothing because Okies had no place to go; once evicted, they could only drift down the road and start another camp. In time, some of the settlements either became or altered existing towns: "Little Oklahoma" or "Little Arkansas" or "Little Texas" became Lamont or East Salinas or Live Oak because the migrants sought decent, stable lives. The transition was not easy, as historian Carey McWilliams points out: "The established towns and cities strenuously resisted petitions to extend roads, sewers, and other facilities to the satellite migrant settlements and regarded annexation as unthinkable."

More than a few Okie families scraped together enough money to establish themselves in a town and enroll their children in school, while the breadwinner continued to follow crops. But even such "respectable" actions were apt to be scorned, since Okies at first contributed little to the tax base, while they placed demands on public services. Education caused the greatest hubbub. Just as southwestern migrants saw schools as their children's best hope of reaping California's rich promise, locals tended to see Okie kids as threats to the quality of school systems. That their children might date or even marry Okies concerned many parents. Moreover, in the schools, migrant children posed a threat to the often unacknowledged but inflexible class structure of rural areas because they were whites in roles traditionally relegated to nonwhites.

One result was that Okies became victims of stereotyping as rigid as other minority groups faced, perhaps even more so, since many people sought means to tell "bad" white folks from "good" ones. The malnourished appearance of migrants was identified as a "racial type": skinny necks with protuberant Adam's apples, concave chests, slumping shoulders, scrawniness in general. They were decried as the lowest subspecies of whites by authorities such as Madera's health director, Lee A. Stone, who wrote that Okies were "a people whose cultural and environmental background is so bad that for a period of more than three hundred years no advance has been made in living conditions among them."

In 1938 the general public became sharply aware of southwestern migrants. First, floods swept large portions of the Central Valley, forcing increased public attention on the plight of the poor, washed-out Okies. Before that, especially in urban

areas, "Okie" had been no more than a word occasionally encountered. Suddenly reports and photographs of the plight of
desperate migrants dominated newspapers, reaching everyone.

And it wasn't only the flood that caused problems. The
Agricultural Adjustment Administration cut California's cotton acreage by over a third that year, intensifying poverty by
lessening opportunities for work. Welfare rolls, both federal
and local, grew; the only true relief came from Farm Security Administration camps and grants. The great oversupply of
laborers—of *people*—created unimagined problems, souring
the previous sweetheart relationship between valley towns and
farm interests, especially large growers.

Because they tended to settle, Okies had quickly acquired
the franchise. And most often they were Southern Democrats
or Populists who voted a straight Democratic ticket. (Ironically,
they did not seem to recognize that they were to some extent victims of New Deal farm policies.) Conservative interests
blamed southwestern migrants to a large degree for the 1938
defeat of their candidate, Frank Merriam, by liberal Culbert
Olson. In fact, conservative power had been on the decline, but
many preferred to accuse the newcomers rather than recognize
the subtle causes long at work in the state. As Stein pointed out,
"The Okies entered a state undergoing major political transfor-
mation and they accelerated changes that might otherwise have
taken years longer to occur." The migrants acted as catalysts—
or the perhaps proverbial straw that temporarily broke the conservative camel's back—but they were no more than that.

Conservative forces, especially members of the Associated
Farmers, began to hatch plans to counter the "invasion" of
California. There was even talk of "repatriation"—the same
ploy that had during the 1930s rid California of nearly 150,000
Mexican farm laborers. In late 1938, growers' organizations and
other business interests organized a major campaign against

the migrants. Kern County's Committee of Sixty soon evolved into the statewide California Citizens Association, ostensibly a spontaneous organization of taxpayers, but in fact something else: The CCA's backers included twenty-seven oil companies, six banking and investing firms, among them Bank of America, and three of the state's largest agribusinesses: Kern County Land Company, DiGiorgio Farms, and Miller and Lux.

Among the CCA's activities was the circulation of a petition demanding that no more relief be distributed to migrants and that the government "aid and encourage the return of the idle thousands" to their home states. By January 1939, 100,000 signatures graced the petition, and many groups had endorsed it. Hovering behind many complaints was not only the fear that Okies would join unions and help organize agricultural labor but also that they would permanently tip the state's political balance away from conservative domination. Because the previously welcomed glut of cheap migrant labor had now become an embarrassment, welfare payments—especially Farm Security Administration grants—were predictably the focus of the CCA's campaign. Thomas McManus, an insurance executive from Bakersfield who became the group's most prominent spokesman, claimed that "No greater invasion by the destitute has ever been recorded in the history of mankind" and that Okies "came from the impoverished submarginal stratum."

One tragedy of the propaganda campaign that developed was that people slowly but certainly began to perceive Okies only in terms of labels. The pro-migrant Simon J. Lubin Society joined the fray too, but for verbal violence nothing rivaled antimigrant hyperbole. Conservative speakers barnstormed the state; radio broadcasts ranted against "Okies, Arkies, and Texies." One famous "letter," destined to be printed later with slight changes to indict Negroes and Mexicans as well, was widely circulated by the Associated Farmers in 1938:

117

Dear Odessa,

You and Coy must try and come to California this fall. We've got everything we want now. We get our relief checks for forty dollars every two weeks and we've bought a new car. We go into town every two weeks and get commodities. That helps a heap on our grocery bill and the case worker comes out and gives the children clothes so that they can keep in school. You sure want to come out.　　　　　　　　　　　　　　—your sister, Bessie

Even the California Chamber of Commerce joined the propaganda war. There had long been gutter stories circulated about the loose morals (and concomitant sexual prowess) of the Okies: rumors of promiscuity and incest were rampant. The August 1938 issue of *California*, the state chamber of commerce's magazine, contained an article by Loring A. Schuler entitled "Dust Bowl Moves to California" that said, in part:

And there is so much unmorality among them—no immorality; they just don't know any better. There was a father who was arrested for outraging his daughter. His whole family appeared in court to defend him, and when he was sent to jail his wife said, "They oughtn't to send paw to jail for that. She's his own property and he can do what he pleases with her."

Charges of immorality had, of course, been leveled at every minority group in the West's long history.

Ironically, while there certainly were some Okies guilty of sexual aberrations, a great many more were old-fashioned, fundamentalist Christians who scorned dancing and makeup and who considered their new California neighbors to be sinful indeed. In many ways, denominations such as the Church of the Nazarene, the Assembly of God, the Pentecostal Holiness, and the Four-Square Gospel acted as major Central Valley links

118

with the old places and old values for displaced Southwest-erners—especially women. Many men were apt to use honky-tonks and country music for the same purpose; they were islands of comfort in an uncomfortable setting. In both cases, it was not long before Okies were developing their own hangouts, whether churches or bars or anything in between.

Another common charge was that Okies were lawless. This grew in part because the newcomers refused to be pushed around and were quick to throw punches if insulted. In another limited, memorable sense—beyond the predictable, poverty-related crime—it was true. There had developed before the mi-gration a Robin Hood syndrome that arose from the frontiers-men's distrust of institution and in part from the Anglo-Saxon tradition of honorable outlaws. Acting outside the law was one recourse that otherwise powerless people had in the face of what they considered an unjust system; a song by Guthrie ended with the damning line: "You won't ever see an outlaw drive a family from their home." You would, of course, see banks and sheriffs do that.

Okie outlaws, often romanticized, appeared throughout the Depression, with Pretty Boy Floyd winning greatest esteem and understanding. Steinbeck's Ma Joad claimed, "I knowed Purty Boy Floyd's ma. He wan't a bad boy. Jes' got drove in a corner."

The final trump card in the propaganda campaign was per-haps most predictable: The migrants were Reds, or at least communist dupes. As is usual, such accusations were prompted by a little truth and lot of bombast, and some of it is just plain funny in retrospect. One organization of "patriots," the Califor-nia Cavaliers, publicly stated: "Anyone who peeps about higher wages will wish he hadn't." Stalin and Hitler couldn't have put it more succinctly.

But the accusations were not funny in the late 1930s when at-tempts to organize farm labor seemed to threaten the traditional balance of power in the fields. There had been strikes in the Central and Imperial valleys in 1933–34, primarily by Mexican and Filipino workers under the banner of the Communist-organized Cannery and Agricultural Workers Industrial Union (CAWIU), which had taken over from Mexican unions. Residents of the Valley were primed for Reds when the second major attempt to unionize occurred in 1938–39.

Perhaps a little less violence and more success could have resulted had the AFL truly involved itself in organizing farm workers, but it did not. One of its spokesmen, Paul Scharrenberg, explained why: "Only fanatics are willing to live in shacks or tents and get their heads broken in the interests of migratory labor." Local AFL units were short of such fanatics, since many of their members had led anti-Okie movements in agricultural communities. It was under the banner of the CIO that a new union, the United Cannery, Agricultural, Packing, and Allied Workers of America (UCAPAWA) finally organized in Arizona and California. Growers and other unions were quick to accuse the new group of being Red: "The Communist CIO combine is attempting to use farm labor as an instrument for halting the flow of crops to the canneries," claimed Edward Vandeleur, secretary of the California Federation of Labor.

Most of the arguments against farm unions offered during recent times were honed during the late 1930s. Not only were the organizers Reds, but the delicate relationships between growers and migrants could tolerate no union interference: "We [farmers] are their friends and they are ours . . . we look out for their interests." Low wages kept food prices low, and unions would ruin that delicate economic balance. Strikes could not be tolerated since farm produce was perishable.

What were the migrants doing through all this? "Okies played a larger role as strikebreakers than as pickets," reports Stein. In fact, after at first harboring illusions that Okies might be the bulwark of the movement, the UCAPAWA actually re-sorted to picketing migrant camps to keep migrants from work-ing. Okies were often starving, sunk to a level of despair at which survival—especially for their children—obviated any theoretical economic or political concerns. They were desper-ate people by the end of the decade. One migrant probably summed up consensus views when he said, "We got enough troubles without going Communist."

Among Woody Guthrie's problems as an alleged Okie spokesman was that he confused his own leftist zeal for general goals. As a result, he remains far more celebrated in Berke-ley's salons than in Bakersfield's saloons. While he was singing pro-union songs, Southwesterners were more apt to be seeking survival at any wage, actually enhancing their image in the eyes of some growers and townspeople by strikebreaking. The final effect of the Okies' coming was to impede the unionization of farm labor.

In 1939 there were approximately 5,600 labor camps in this state, and Carey McWilliams had been appointed chief of the California Division of Immigration and Housing, an ominous appointment indeed in the eyes of growers and anti-Okie groups. McWilliams, they understood, was intent on enforcing the long-ignored Labor Camp Act to make condi-tions decent for migrants. Then, that spring, Steinbeck's *The Grapes of Wrath* dropped like a bomb from its publishers, and conservative groups howled. Kern County's Board of Super-visors became infamous for banning the novel. In a futile at-tempt to counter Steinbeck, pro-grower books, films, and pam-phlets were rushed into print, including *Of Human Kindness, The Grapes of Gladness, Plums of Plenty*, and other forget-table epics.

Later in 1939, a revised edition of McWilliams's classic *Fac-tories in the Fields* was released, and conservative outrage ex-

121

ploded. There had to be a conspiracy, it was claimed, and McWilliams was called "Agricultural Pest No. 1, outranking pear blight and boll weevil." In fact, the two authors had not conspired—they didn't even know one another—but both had been appalled by the excesses of California's agribusiness and the exploitation of southwestern migrants.

A tense couple of years remained for Okies until wartime prosperity took economic pressure off them. As McWilliams pointed out, "Three wars in the Pacific within the span of a single generation accomplished wonders for most Californians, including [Steinbeck's] Joads." As migrant George Watson explained, "We moved to Oakland and worked in the shipyards for two years and saved every dime we could lay our hands on." His family then bought a Central Valley farm.

A tough, able people, the Okies have moved a long way from those ditch banks of the 1930s. They are prominent in state and local government, in all professions, and whether they have chosen to join the state's mainstream or remain displaced Southwesterners, they are proud of their survival. The place they settled most densely, the southern end of the Central Valley, has been profoundly altered by their presence.

In 1983, Butch and Linda Stewart and their family followed the path that Steinbeck's Joad family had taken nearly fifty years earlier. "We came across country in U-Haul trucks. When we got to this valley, we'd been on the road for three days, 105, 106, 107 degrees, and the baby was cross," says Linda. "I know we looked like death warmed over. . . . And this little old couple sat down and said, 'Now where are you from, Texas?' And just sat there and helped me get little David satisfied. It was real homey feeling," she admits.

"I would ask, 'Where are you from?' and they would either say, 'I was raised right here . . .' or they would name Oklahoma, Louisiana, Texas, or Arkansas. You don't hear a lot of southern accents, but you have a very southern, very friendly flavor."

Vast numbers of "Dust Bowlers" have entered the middle class here. For every erstwhile Okie, Arkie, or Texie unable to escape poverty and every one rolling in money, there are hundreds, maybe thousands, working, paying their taxes, sending their kids to school, going to church, doing the work that keeps the Valley operating. They are shapers of the new California where biscuits and gravy are easy to order in cafes, where country music and stock-car races and western boots are common. A few migrants have resisted California, but most have joined it and have changed it as well. As Frances Walker, on the porch of her home in Keyes, just south of Modesto, says proudly, "The Okies were invincible. They won. They are here, they own land, homes, and are comfortable. Their children are here and their grandchildren. . . . I'm part of it."

What of the next generation, the California-born children of those first Okie youngsters? A sixth-grader says brightly, "Oh, my dad used to be an Okie." He smiles, for he is, of course, a Californian.

It has become increasingly clear in recent years that the Okie epic was an early, more intense version of what many poor people—whites and nonwhites—have experienced since. When the Okie bard Merle Haggard sings, "I take a lot of pride in what I am," evoking the self-esteem of his gritty, hardworking people, he celebrates our shared humanity.

Oil Town Rumble:
The Young Men
of Taft

I N 1954, I emerged from the visitors' dressing room at Taft High School to see a crowd surging over the parking lot. Having just lost a tough football game, I was in a mood to join the action, so I jostled my way to the throng's core. There I found a pugnacious white youth from Bakersfield pounding a small local. "Fight back, you asshole," a white kid seeing a fight said, "I'm a nigger! I'm a nigger!" That the Bakersfield boy came from a town that could take little justified pride in its own racial relations was of no consequence: He had found an excuse to pick a fight.

Taft has long carried the cross of its Ku Klux Klan past even among its tainted neighbors. In 1975, after thirteen black athletes were run out of town by a mob of white hooligans, much of the nation viewed Taft the same way. But the town's sorry events that year were as much a measure of its well-intended but inept present as of its racist past.

This community grew in the southwestern corner of the Great Central Valley, near Elk Hills and about forty miles west of Bakersfield, an arid region called the Westside Desert, or just the Westside. The location offered virtually no water in dry years but sat over a vast reservoir of petroleum. Called "Moron" for a time—something that events in 1975 seemed to have rendered prophetic—Taft served as trading center for the enormously rich Midway-Sunset oil field. It was described in 1912 as "perhaps the liveliest town in the state," a frontier community of the sort that movie fans once expected Spencer Tracy and Clark Gable to brawl in. Beer was for a time actually cheaper than water in Taft, which was populated largely by young men during its early years, young men given to male diversions. It may not have been sex, drugs, and rock 'n' roll, but beer, brawls, and bordellos kept Taft busy; casual violence was a way of life.

Taft was incorporated in 1910, and its development has been closely linked with the social history of California's oil industry, for oil companies owned not only much of the surrounding land but a good chunk of the community as well. Both the town and its immediate area have a long history of absentee ownership, thus many locals have a brooding sense of distant, often faceless big shots controlling their destiny.

Nonwhites have been even more absent than owners, for

until the recent past, oil jobs in Central California were white men's work. Moreover, many of those who have labored on the hot, treeless hills around Taft drifted there from other oil areas, often from the South and Southwest. It was asserted during the lilywhite past when Negroes were not hired in Kern County's oil fields that they didn't even want jobs there; the work was too much for them—only white men possessed the qualities necessary for such demanding labor. So both Taft and the oil fields grew up all white.

While some "No colored allowed" signs are reported to have been posted, the town's reputation was enough to discourage most nonwhites. It was accepted during my youth that no Negro should allow himself to be found in Taft after dusk, and everyone talked about, but no one ever saw, a sign—"Nigger don't let the sun set on you here"—that was supposed to have been posted on the city limits. The same tales were told about other Valley towns that grew around oil: Coalinga, Avenal, Oildale.

Precisely because they had isolated themselves from non-whites, many residents of Taft were poorly prepared for the rise in black pride and consciousness during the 1960s. Their ignorance easily festered into fear and hate. But in 1965, Taft was integrated because another local tradition, athletic excellence, was in jeopardy.

Despite the town's small size (about 4,200), both Taft High School and Taft Junior College had reputations as tough competitors that held their own against much larger schools. But when the oil business began to automate and employ smaller crews, and some surrounding "feeder areas" such as Cuyama, Fellows, and Maricopa began drying up, the junior college in particular found itself drawing from a diminishing population. Taft High was forced to drop out of the large-school league in which it had long competed effectively and play a schedule of smaller schools. The local college, with only about 400 students among the state's smallest, refused to become a loser.

Although it had to leave the state junior college athletic association and play an intersectional schedule, Taft J.C. began to import athletes, black as well as white. In 1956 the Cougars had managed an unbeaten season with a team of local kids. Nine years later, large numbers of outsiders were enlisted to bolster the school's gridiron prowess. And bolster they did: In the years following out-of-state recruitment, Cougar football teams have been nationally ranked a number of times and have won several bowl games.

However, the presence of players recruited from elsewhere quickly became a wedge between a segment of the town and the college. Said a Taft resident, "There are some people in the community who feel the district ought to spend money on its own people." One participant in the May 1975 violence, a high-school dropout, acknowledged that black athletes had been a special sore spot. "They replace local athletes," he asserted, claiming that they also receive an unfair share of campus grants and jobs. Tom Harrell, then athletic director and head football coach, disagreed. He confirmed that without the imported athletes the team couldn't remain competitive. Taft had returned to the California association and played in a tough conference.

College officials had, moreover, long seen the recruitment of black athletes as an important part of the school's educational mission. They enrolled other nonwhites, many of them foreign exchange students, as a means of introducing local youngsters to the complexity of a multiethnic world. Taft J.C. also introduced a small ethnic studies program, but was unable to reach dropouts and those marginal or poor people who moved directly from high school to the oil field jobs, or to no jobs at all, then smoldered while others—many of them outsiders—used the local college as a step toward richer lives.

Since Taft had no black girls for young men to go out with, interracial dating has been a predictable problem, for few of the imported athletes were celibate. Indeed, thugs cited a rumor that a white girl was pregnant by a black athlete as one cause of Taft's violent days in May. A combination of intolerance on the part of some Taftians and naivete on the part of college officials must be blamed. Studies have shown that sexual tension is considerably reduced on campuses when relatively equal numbers of nonwhite men and women are enrolled in schools, and not because interracial dating lessens significantly. Apparently the college community relaxes when everyone—male and female, black and white—shares the opportunity to date freely.

Taft and the area around it had long been known as fighting country, a place where men young and old test their masculinity in direct physical confrontations. The town's police chief, Walter McKee, said, "Taft is notorious rough country. This is an oil town. Heck, we have a dozen fights some nights."

But the incidents that erupted on May 25, 1975, constituted far more than mere fights, a fact that Chief Mckee seemed to have trouble understanding. At about 5 P.M. that day, a large group of young white men confronted three black students on Center Street. Police were called and the dispute was aborted.

Little more than an hour later, the same three black athletes were walking from the apartment of one toward the college's residence hall when they were first hemmed in, then chased, by five carloads of whites. Finally surrounded, the three fought back as best they could, and an attacker, Doug Henry, was shot in the neck. Joe Rhone, one of the beleaguered jocks, was swinging a case containing a shotgun when the weapon discharged, wounding Henry, who was armed and had cut Rhone in the assault.

The three young men finally managed to escape and flee to the college's dormitory, where they called the police. They were placed in protective custody. Rhone and a white man were later arrested, the former for attempted murder, the latter for disturbing the peace. Charges against the black athlete were eventually dropped.

But the evening was young, and Henry's friends easily increased their number to an estimated sixty once word was passed that Doug had been "shot by a nigger." The mob stormed the campus yelling, "Kill the niggers!" Most blacks wisely hid until police could be once more summoned, but one football player tried to reason with the crowd, only to find himself literally running for his life until a white teammate rescued him in a car.

The white athlete's action did not escape notice—and another dimension was added to events. Word soon circulated that it was us (the hardworking townies) against them (the college nigger lovers). Eventually, all blacks trapped within the dorm were also taken into protective custody, and they were escorted to nearby Bakersfield.

Two days later, after many incidents in which cruising rowdies abused students—"a continuing reign of terror," one resident called it—Dennis McCall, editor of Taft's *Daily Midway Driller*, was assaulted by a local named Rick Riddick. White ruffians had become incensed by the slim, bespectacled McCall's reporting of and editorial comment on the earlier incident. Riddick accosted him, knocked him down, and kicked him. Nearby students claimed they couldn't aid the fallen man because one of Riddick's pals leveled a gun at them.

The assailant was arrested three days later and was eventually convicted of assault and battery, fined $250, and placed on probation. He would certainly have received a stiffer sentence, but McCall, knowing that Riddick had a wife and two children, asked that he not be jailed. The convicted man's response to McCall's generosity reveals much about both the limited insight and unlimited sense of victimization that characterized many of the whites involved.

"Hell, it wasn't nothin' but a fistfight," he is reported to have said. "He told 'em not to put me in jail, and when someone has that much stroke, you know what that can do." One sad attribute of the rowdies is that most remain convinced that *they* are victims. Because many of them weren't sufficiently motivated or bright to make it in school, because others weren't swift or supple enough to excel at athletics, because they found themselves denied even the hoary illusion that they were intrinsically superior to blacks, they cracked.

And here, at last, is the heart of Taft's problems. How does a community—especially one with Taft's history—reach people whose self-concept is so blurred or distorted that they lash out like frightened animals? The men who perpetrated Taft's terror last May were not evil, though their actions were. No, they were frustrated, perhaps uncomprehending products of an upwardly mobile society in which they had failed to rise; like men stuck in quicksand, they flailed in desperation, and their actions harmed not only their community but their nation as well.

By the time Riddick was convicted, only six of sixty dormitory residents remained at Taft Junior College. Many others refused to return to campus and subject themselves to further abuse. College officials acted quickly, making arrangements for students who would not return to school to take final examinations and housing remaining dorm residents with faculty and staff personnel (many of whom then received threatening

130

phone calls). The Westside College District Board of Trustees demanded a full-scale investigation by both local police and the city council. Kern County's grand jury also began probing the incident.

As more and more facts about the sad events of May became public, local opinion mounted against the assailants. Deputy sheriff Charles Scott, a college trustee, publicly characterized the attacks as the work of "a small segment of thugs." Taft College dean of students Ray Matthai told a large audience at a public meeting, "We have had two nights of hell and that is an experience we don't care to go through again."

More surprising, a reaction even developed within the ranks of the attackers, some of whom came to see that they had been lied to and used. One young man wrote a letter to the *Daily Midway Driller*, apologizing for his part in the violence and admitting that he had acted upon hearsay which he "later discovered was totally unfounded."

Long before national media focused attention on Taft's crisis, residents were taking steps to avert future strife. Local police approached the FBI, and word was also passed to the Civil Rights Division of the Justice Department. Angel Alderette, a department official, promised after visiting Taft, "Law enforcement officials and interested folk are going to see that this doesn't happen again." His agency sent a community relations team and offered to help develop a contingency plan for reintegration. To the hooligans who had created the problem, Alderette's comments were direct and low-key: "This is not going to be allowed."

Local authorities, stung and confused by the criticism they received, said they knew who the miscreants were and were ready for them. "We weren't prepared for the trouble when it started," acknowledged deputy sheriff Scott; "I think we can guarantee protection now." Moreover, both the FBI and the

Justice Department also knew who the troublemakers were and exactly where to look if further problems developed. Doug Henry's disingenuous prediction—"If they [Blacks] come back . . . somebody is going to get killed"—widely reprinted in the press, promised to boomerang.

Taft's police force was especially bombarded for its slow, indecisive response to the outbreak of terrorism. Chief McKee attempted to deflect criticism with inept explanations. He said events were "blown out of proportion" and told one reporter that Joe Rhone had been arrested because police "didn't want to be responsible for not arresting anyone." When college officials criticized police for their ineffectiveness, McKee responded, "It looks like they are trying to find someone else to blame." He also admitted past disagreements with college officials. "The community is overreacting," he opined, "and as usual the police are to blame."

If his public statements accurately reflected McKee's perception of events, he seemed unable to distinguish roughnecks tussling in a local bar and an incipient lynch mob bent on racial violence. The chief had a local reputation as a tough professional and one has to hope he was simply caught off-guard by May's violence, then let his mouth outrun his mind. In any case, a town with Taft's strong tax base could afford high-quality law enforcement and soon moved in that direction.

Predictably, Taft's citizens were defensive following the town's condemnation by national media. Wrote one local man to the *Daily Midway Driller*: "It is the kind of incident that happens many times daily in the city." He did not say which city, but he did go on to blame "irresponsible news media" for having "blown the incident completely out of proportion." But such arguments, no matter how heartfelt, were empty; no one with any knowledge of America's history could miss the symbolic horror of a white mob running all the blacks from town.

It was not long before thoughtful citizens recognized and explored the real problem. Wrote Shirley M. Daly in a letter to the editor: "It's true we have been shamed—not by the articles in the newspapers but by the actions of some of our citizens." In another letter, to the *Daily Midway Driller*, Irene Ramos Fairhurst pointed out that Taft's crisis would not disappear: "It's like cancer. Do you just let it alone and hope it goes away or do you get help and treat it?" In an open letter, Jerry Peavyhouse, president of the chamber of commerce, asked that the "whole town not be judged by the actions of a few people."

Bonnie Beaty, who had long opened her home to out-of-town athletes, examined what such youngsters bring to Taft: "a different form of wealth—a richness and variety of ethnic cultures that comprise the rest of America and the world, and their unique qualities as individuals." Mrs. Beaty, who recognized that some of Taft's problems stemmed from the fact that people there knew so little about nonwhites, concluded by saying, "We may be a small town but we don't have to be small-minded too."

Most significantly, perhaps, all the above-listed remarks, plus many more, were published in the local paper. Taft's residents did not hide behind anonymous letters but openly stated their opposition to mob rule and racism. A large number also cooperated in circulating a petition outlining to the city council steps they felt were necessary to correct the damage.

Taft College publicly invited black students to return—thirteen enrolled the following fall, but not all were returnees—and considerably beefed up its security. Said board president Ray Zak: "From our standpoint—even if nothing else is accomplished in the community—we will make it [the campus] a more secure and safer place for our students." There were no more incidents after school reopened in September.

There were, however, still rumblings in Taft's beer bars and drive-ins where clusters of flawed people gathered to assure one another that only physical violence was manly and that "runnin' the niggers off" was patriotic. But no one knew better than the youthful rowdies and their middle-aged adolescent sympathizers that the town they claimed to defend was against them. Taft was no guerrilla enclave of racists that would hide offenders. It was a community trying desperately to outgrow its past.

One of the first black athletes to attend Taft College, Ray Stubblefield, recalled that shortly after he arrived in town during the mid-1960s, he and three other black students sought to attend a movie downtown. A car full of white men passed them and its occupants commented about "niggers on the street." When the car returned, Stubblefield and friends refused to be bullied, so the malcontents emerged with chains and clubs. "About that time," he recalls, "many of the middle-class whites from Taft—some college students—also stopped their cars. Fortunately, they came to aid us by surrounding the white troublemakers."

It wasn't Stubblefield's only trouble in Taft, but it symbolized for him what was hopeful in the town. He felt strongly enough to write a long letter to the *Daily Midway Driller* in June of 1975 expressing one black man's faith in the good people of Taft. With the eyes of America on them, they had to once more surround troublemakers, but the town's underlying social and economic problems would not be easily overcome, for they were and are the nation's.

William Saroyan and the Critics

I N FRESNO, where William Saroyan kept two cluttered tract houses during the final years of his life, his closest chum, Varzat Samuelian Mektrichi, is working on a sixteen-foot statue of the author. Varzat explains the jumble of his own studio in a broad accent: "If it be clean, it don't be artist's place. It be restaurant, maybe, or bank."

"Willie" Saroyan would agree heartily, for his own work-places were never confused with restaurants or banks. With disaster areas, maybe.

135

He actually used one of his Fresno houses to store posses-sions, while he lived in the other, described by Bob Sector as "a typical tract-type home with a mad tangle of sunflowers, weeds and fruit trees in the yard. . . . The inside of his house was just as disheveled, a mishmash of books strewn everywhere." And Saroyan's Paris apartment was "systematically disorganized," according to Dickran Kouymijian.

The same has been said of Saroyan's literary philosophy. He was very much his own man. Critic Robert Kirsch noted that Saroyan believed that if he wrote enough, something interest-ing or intelligible would eventually come out of it. It did. Also some things magical and unique and controversial.

Few American writers have risen as fast or tumbled as dra-matically as William Saroyan. There were many reasons for this beyond his disordered output, not the least of which was his personality. To some, Saroyan's self-centered, sometimes abrasive character became more important than his writing. He was, during the first half of his career, as much a public figure as an artist. The confusion of those two roles—by him as well as by critics—made it easy to ignore his literary accomplish-ments once his notoriety faded. At the end of his life, he was reclusive, having retreated into Fresno's Armenian-American community.

An artist's psychological contradictions are finally much less important than the quality of his art, and from his first pub-lished volume (*The Daring Young Man on the Flying Trapeze and Other Stories*, 1934) until his last (*Obituaries*, 1979)—both of which were cited as among their years' best books—Saroyan was an authentic, singular American genius. He was also his own biggest fan, a fact that offended critics and readers alike.

A major factor, probably *the* major factor, in the Fresno native's fall from critical grace was the adversarial relationship he had developed with critics. He wrote in 1940:

What is lacking in . . . criticism is the fullness and humanity of understanding which operates in myself, in my work, and in my regard for others. . . . Consequently, it is difficult for them to make sense in themselves of that which is complicated and unusual for them. What should enlarge them because of its understanding, drives them more completely behind the fort of their own limitations.

Little wonder he was a prime candidate for literary ostracism.

Today, with his personality no longer a factor, Saroyan's art is enjoying critical reevaluation. It, not his ego or pugnaciousness or reclusiveness, is at issue, and it stands up very well indeed. As David Kheridan recently observed:

His writing had a quality of innocence and eagerness and wonder about a moment—any moment of living—that made us feel more alive ourselves—more alive, that is, than we actually were, but for this very reason it made us yearn and stretch and seek a way to grow.

After World War II, Saroyan fell with a thud from critical fashion. Not only were the books he published attacked but—more remarkably—his earlier achievements were, until recently at least, ignored or slighted, making him a kind of literary nonperson. "Saroyan has been patronized and under-interpreted," asserts H. W. Matalene. Even in his native West, his accomplishments were neglected, although much of his best writing was set there. *My Heart's in the Highlands, The Time of Your Life,* and *Hello Out There,* Saroyan's three finest plays, employed distinctly western settings and tones. He was very much a writer of his time, of his place, and of his dynamic cultural blend, Armenian-American.

Add to his distinguished dramas such stories as "The Daring

Young Man on the Flying Trapeze," "The Pomegranate Trees," and "Seventy Thousand Assyrians," and Saroyan's position in American letters should be secure. Few twentieth-century American authors have produced a richer, more diverse body of work. Unfortunately, he also produced more than his share of mediocre-to-poor material, and by the end of his life his original optimism had become anachronistic.

At his best, Saroyan straddled the worlds of high and folk culture, investing what he wrote with great immigrant energy, merging class and ethnicity in occasionally crude, frequently irresistible literature that captured the power of the upwardly mobile poor; he produced a kind of writing possible only in the U.S.A. There is reason to believe that Saroyan may be remembered as the most uniquely American writer of his time precisely because he never forgot what it was to be an immigrant in a nation of immigrants, and because he was never deflected by the abstract concerns of intellectuals.

Mary McCarthy, early in Saroyan's career, pinpointed a source of both his greatest art and, perhaps, some of his problems with the literary establishment. "He still retains his innocence," she observed. When he died on May 19, 1981, in Fresno, Saroyan had won both the New York Drama Critics Circle Award and the Pulitzer Prize for *The Time of Your Life* (the first writer to be so doubly honored), an Academy Award for *The Human Comedy,* and the California Gold Medal for *Tracy's Tiger.* He was elected to the National Institute of Arts and Letters, and later became one of the initial inductees to the Theater Hall of Fame.

William Saroyan emerged as a writer during the Great Depression, while America was in the throes of a national loss of faith and questioning of values. Although many critics had trouble accepting his optimistic, original stories, readers did not. He talked and wrote about the human spirit. That Saroyan also turned down his Pulitzer Prize certainly did little to raise his stock among literary insiders. His behavior, like some of his writing, seemed downright unliterary. As novelist Herbert Gold wrote following Saroyan's death, "He wanted, very boy- ishly, just to knock everyone's eyes out with beauty and fun and delight."

Born in Fresno in 1908, Saroyan was placed in an Oakland orphanage at the age of three following the death of his father, a poet and ordained minister. Four years later, his family re- united and returned to Fresno where he grew up. Experiences that would later resurface as rich literary material in such books as *Little Children* (1937) and *My Name is Aram* (1940) marked the remainder of Saroyan's childhood. He worked at odd jobs, rubbing elbows with a lively group of people of all ethnic types, developed earthy rural values, and was always assured of the support of his extended family and of the Armenian commu- nity. He did not graduate from high school.

Small wonder that Saroyan's work evidences little social or intellectual pretension, so it is accessible to a large audience. He also refused to be limited; in "Seventy Thousand Assyri- ans" his protagonist says: "I am an Armenian . . . I have no idea what it's like to be an Armenian . . . I have a faint idea what it's like to be alive. That's the only thing that interests me greatly." That is, while everything he wrote was influenced by his Armenian, poor, Central Valley heritage, that influence emerges from within rather than being imposed from without. When he tells the truth well enough, it is everyone's.

In 1928, while working in San Francisco, Saroyan pub- lished a story in *Overland Monthly and Outwest Magazine* and decided to make writing his career. Six years later his first book, *The Daring Young Man on the Flying Trapeze and Other Stories,* was published; an acknowledged classic, the title story remains a gem in a collection that was fresh, zany, and highly individualistic. "Try to be alive," the author advised in his preface. "You will be dead soon enough." If the book exhibited many of the considerable strengths that were to mark Saroyan as a cutting-edge artist unconcerned with established literary forms, many of those same innovative tales were viewed by some critics as undisciplined. Today, they seem ahead of their time. Saroyan's response to Eric Bentley's complaint about careless writing perhaps sums up his attitude: "One cannot expect an Armenian to be an Englishman."

Whatever its source—the writer's ethnicity, his unsystematic self-education, his early poverty, his Valley upbringing— Saroyan showed during the 1930s a vivacity and originality that seemed exactly correct for that period. Having emerged from a region where life was *always* tough for the poor, and having survived personal hard times, he was not overwhelmed by the general malaise. "I cannot resist the temptation to mock any law which is designated to hamper the spirit of man," he wrote in an early story. Critics of that period, burdened by polemic proletarian positions or reconsidering the power of naturalism, didn't know how to treat this brash Californian. Of late, critics are acknowledging that Saroyan was a literary master, not a naif.

By the beginning of World War II, the Fresnan estimated that he had written more than 500 tales. His craft had progressed, and he began to evince a profound sense of place in his fiction. Increasingly in his work—especially in the superb *My Name Is Aram*—Saroyan returned to Fresno and the Valley for both setting and subject. He used characters and situations to greater, sometimes magical effect, for the stories were not self-centered; as Howard Floan suggests, "If Saroyan had not discovered the literary uses of Fresno and the Valley, he could not have given us the best of his short stories—nor his plays."

Another important influence on Saroyan's writing was the oral tradition with which he was raised. He explained:

> Everything I write, everything I have ever written, is allegorical. This came to pass inevitably. One does not choose to write allegorically any more than one chooses to grow black hair on his head. The stories of Armenia . . . are all allegorical, and apart from the fact that I heard these stories as a child . . . I myself am a product of Asia Minor, hence the allegorical and the real are closely related in my mind.
>
> In fact all reality to me is allegorical.

When in 1939 he converted his short story "The Man with His Heart in the Highlands" into the play *My Heart's in the Highlands,* he demonstrated his comfort with spoken language, as well as his allegorical bent. The play was successful, and even his detractors agreed that the Californian had provided a radical departure from usual theatrical fare. Both George Jean Nathan and John Mason Brown considered it the finest Broadway play of the 1938–39 season.

The following year Saroyan produced one of the classic dramas of the modern American theater, *The Time of Your Life.* It confirmed what the author's earlier dramatic work had hinted, that he was as original and irreverent on stage as he was in print. Nona Balakian points out that "nothing quite so informal and spontaneous had happened on the American stage before Saroyan came along." Certainly the play illustrated his quest, stated earlier in a short story: "If I want to do anything I want to speak a more universal language, the heart of man, the unwritten part of man, that which is eternal and common to all races."

From his first published book, Saroyan evidenced a freedom from conventional literary modes of reality that marks him today as an early exemplar of what has been called Magical Realism. Merged levels of consciousness, powerful intuition, little concern for chronological time—such elements led Edmund Wilson to praise "magical feats" that he said "are accomplished by the enchantment of Saroyan's temperament, which induces us to take from him a good many things that we should not accept from other people." Another giant of American criticism, John Mason Brown, proclaimed, "Saroyan managed to widen the theater's horizons by escaping from facts and reason." It has been too easy of late to dismiss Saroyan's optimism as dated while ignoring his magic; "The Daring Young Man on the Flying Trapeze" places him firmly in the front ranks of American magical realists.

The Californian produced two of his most successful novels during World War II, *The Human Comedy* and *The Adventures of Wesley Jackson*. The latter was a picaresque version of army life with a somewhat hard edge which Wilson admired; finally, however, Wilson scored the novel because he believed Saroyan succumbed to "the impulse toward self-befuddling and self-protective fantasy." *The Human Comedy* began as an award-winning screenplay and soon became the focus of a drama itself when Saroyan tried to buy back rights to it from Metro-Goldwyn-Mayer. Failing, he retreated to write a play, *Get Away Old Man*, that dramatized his conflict with the studio. But if Saroyan got the final word, MGM seems to have managed the final laugh; *Get Away Old Man* flopped.

Following the war, Saroyan went into a critical tailspin. Disillusioned by his army experience, tax problems, and the collapse of his two marriages to Carol Marcus, his mood and literature darkened. By his own admission, he drank too much and gambled too much. "Three years in the army and a stupid marriage had all but knocked me out of the picture and, if the truth be told, out of life itself."

Saroyan gradually brought his drinking and gambling under control, and once more began producing high-quality work. But, critically at least, it was too late. As Matalene points out:

> One senses that critics have been less interested in discovering and teaching Saroyan's message than they have been in congratulating themselves for having been so democratic as to have admitted to the canon of recognized literature the work of an uneducated, penniless Armenian from Fresno—at least for as long as he seems amusing.

He no longer seemed amusing, or perhaps life had generally darkened for everyone, so he was dropped like the outsider he always was.

During the final years of his life he produced several entertaining, often prolix, memoirs, one of which, *Not Dying* (1963), led Herbert Mitgang to observe in the *New York Times*: "Saroyan shows that he can be more in the vanguard than many of the official literary-map personages in *Esquire* . . . he'll be around long after this year's hipsters have become next year's squares." Saroyan's mood was often morose in his later years; he seemed preoccupied by death. Barry Gifford and Lawrence Lee in their sensitive study, *Saroyan: A Biography* (1984), quote the Fresnan: "The world is a great big fat falsehood."

One balanced assessment of Saroyan's personality has recently been offered in *My Name Is Saroyan* by his friend and associate James H. Tashjian:

> There is little question that Saroyan's personal conduct was in direct contradiction of his father's rigid code—Saroyan gambled

and gamboled, he was flaky and notoriously unreliable, he drank heavily on occasion, wenched and was twice divorced—all mis-virtues. . . . But he was, at the same time, a dedicated pacifist, a ridiculer of the goosestep, a foe of peonage and patronage. He was impatient of dissimulation, generous and charitable . . . and was respectful of all religions.

Clearly, the Fresno loner was a flawed, passionate man, a com-plicated mixture of virtue and vice whose great talent magnified all aspects of his personality.

Aram Saroyan (in *William Saroyan*, 1983), Gifford and Lee, and Tashjian all agree that a major element in William Saroy-an's makeup was the early death of his father, Armenak, a subject he returned to both directly and indirectly throughout his literary career. It "forged in him a basic Oedipal urge—to find the father who had left him," Tashjian points out. "This was to grow into a veritable passion in his manhood. It colored his thoughts and his career." Saroyan's most touching work on this subject is "Armenak of Bitlis" (*Letters from 54 rue Taitbout*, 1969), which tells of a visit to his father's grave in San Jose, then leads the author to recount a sterile meeting with his own son in New York. It is a powerful piece that illustrates well both the writer's personal problems and his continuing abilities.

Sham remained a continuing concern of Saroyan's. Early in his career, he had lamented the influence of tastemakers such as literary critics this way:

> It's wonderful to get up in the morning and go out for a little walk and smell the trees and see the streets and the kids going to school and the clouds in the sky. . . . This is a nice world. So why do they make all the trouble?

Late in his career, once he had become somewhat reclusive, his tone changed. "Can a society which has thrived on lies be expected to survive?" he asked. He answered himself this way: "Possibly, but the people of that society can't be expected not to be grotesque."

Still, flashes of the old spirit surfaced. In a 1978 interview with Gold, Saroyan remarked, "I'm growing old! I'm falling apart! And it's *very interesting!*" He worked out of those two tract houses and rode around Fresno on a bicycle. An eleven-year-old neighbor remembered, "I saw him ridin' with no hands and everything, lots of times." He was a great favorite of neighborhood children, and they were favorites of his.

Bella Stumbo, in the *Los Angeles Times,* added that he "refused all interviews with the press (on the grounds that the 'knotheads' asked him stupid questions), and even turned down invitations to the White House in later years." Shortly before his death, Saroyan called the Associated Press to leave a statement for posthumous release: "Everybody has got to die, but I have always believed an exception would be made in my case. Now what?" Following Saroyan's demise, a memorial service was held in Paris. His Holiness, Vasken I, Catholicos of all Armenians, eulogized the author, calling him "the prodigy of the nation."

In a booklet in the Western Writers Series, *William Saroyan* (1984), Edward Hulsey Foster offers this accurate assessment of the Fresnan's impact on this nation: "Saroyan was one of few welcome breaks in that grey literary landscape portraying and preaching social obligation and reform." Matalene has provided a reasonable summary of Saroyan's career:

[A]ware, in a way that most left-leaning intellectuals in America are not, of the absurdity of existing political, economic, and social arrangements and of the grave moral risks of changing them, Saroyan at his best has remained a prophet without honor in his country.

Fortunately, that is changing, and Saroyan's importance is being acknowledged. Asked a headline in the *San Francisco Chronicle*, "Genius or Ego-Giant?" "Both" is the answer; they are not mutually exclusive categories. In American literary criticism a writer's best work is traditionally employed to assess his or her achievement. When the Fresnan's is evaluated in this manner, its importance is undeniable. He remains literally without peer, this immodest, this exuberant, this original American writer.

Just as he always predicted.

Remembering Hutch

A COUPLE OF years ago, W. H. Hutchinson said to me with a deep chuckle, "These 'golden years' aren't all they're cracked up to be—it's like being nibbled to death by ducks." Well, the ducks took their final nibble at that eminent historian, biographer, and longtime *San Francisco Chronicle* columnist last March, and they tore a pretty good chunk out of those of us who loved him too.

My introduction to Hutch, the curmudgeon who would become one of my special pals, came with a telephone call twenty or so years ago, after I had, in print, indulged in some trendy generalizations. I lifted the receiver, said hello, then heard a gravelly voice: "Quiero hablar a don Geraldo Haslam."

The unexpected Spanish stopped me. Finally I said, "Soy Haslam."

"Well, my young friend," the voice announced, "this is Hutchinson. How in the arrogant pluperfect hell do you justify the Solomonic judgments in your recent felonious assault against wisdom and good taste? Who're you to create an impersonal Moloch out of the hard labor of pioneers?"

The attack dazzled me and my response was feeble. He had slapped leather and I had flinched.

What I couldn't know at the time was that the whole performance—the Spanish, the allusions, the unlikely vocabulary, all of it—was classic Hutchinson and that he was in the habit of confronting those he considered guilty of literary or historical crimes.

When I eventually met my erstwhile adversary, he appeared to be an aging gunfighter: All angles and bones, dressed in a snap-button denim shirt, jeans, and western boots. On his head was a felt cowboy hat that looked as though stew had recently been cooked in it. His face was a sun-punished prune; as he would later observe, "I may or may not look like a hundred miles of bad road, but I always avoid the highway department."

He looked, in fact, exactly like what he chose to be, a man who lived by an earlier but by no means simpler code than most of us. William Henry Hutchinson was at once the most contrary son of a bitch and the most compassionate and considerate guy I've ever known. He would argue over the economics of the rice industry, whether or not bunchgrass turned gray or tan during drought, and he would argue over whether or not he was arguing. He would also give selflessly of his possessions, his time, and his energy.

148

As both a writer and a man, Hutch was direct, hardheaded, and never devious. Writer Robert Speer remembers him as "a refreshing anachronism: a colorful, sharp-tongued, deeply knowledgeable vestige of the West that once was." Often mistaken for an arch-conservative by the arch-liberals who dominate literary life, Hutchinson was in fact more of an iconoclast, his philosophy formed during the Great Depression and honed by lean years after World War II when he struggled to support his family as a freelance writer. "I've gone through life," he explained last year, "saying 'From the bigots of the left and fanatics of the right, may good God deliver the Republic.' I walk down the middle and I get shot at from both sides. A man with those enemies can't be all good." He winked, and his laughter echoed up from some deep internal cavern.

When he was writing his "One Man's West" columns for the *Chronicle*, Hutch's work retained a straightforward frontier feel that was part of that paper's heritage. No reader ever doubted where the writer stood: Of *The Authentic Life of Billy, the Kid* by Pat Garret and Ash Upson, he noted, it "reflects again a morbid preoccupation with him who has been dubbed 'Faust in America' and who was in all truth a buck-toothed, murderous little thug."

Of William H. Leckie's *The Buffalo Soldiers:* "[Negro Cavalrymen] were a spearhead of settlement in the last American frontier, and their desertion rates, their ratio of Medal of Honor winners, and their casualty lists make more publicized Army units look a little pallid. . . . Their record enhances the heritage of all Americans, and this is made pungently clear in Dr. Leckie's history."

So who was this critic and what qualified him to make such distinct judgments? William Henry Hutchinson was born in Denver in 1911. In his youth, he worked as a horse wrangler, cowboy, boiler fireman, and mine mucker, and lessons

149

he learned then did not leave him, as he wrote in "One Man's West":

> I was taught to handle rifle and short gun and shotgun by men whose pigmentation was noticeably darker than my own. I learned what little I know about horses and cattle as a gringo in an essentially Mexican cow outfit. This is a damned good way to shed the shackles of ethnocentricism. . . . I learned to judge my fellows of whatever sex by what they did, not by what they said.

After duty in World War II, he left a good job with a shipping line and repaired to rural Cohasset in Butte County, where he embarked on his writing career. He would pen everything from what he described as "penny-dreadful" westerns to serious studies of the frontier to books in the Gene Autry juvenile novel series. Later, when he had become a well-known author, he was asked to list what he had published earlier and he responded, "I have no accurate bibliography of the several millions of words of mine that have appeared in print. I didn't keep one, for it seemed unimportant then. What counted was whether what I wrote provided sustenance for me and mine. It did." He believed deeply in the sacrality of honest labor, whether with a shovel or a typewriter.

By 1956, he had become an acknowledged authority on the American West, and that year his biography of Eugene Manlove Rhodes, *A Bar Cross Man*, earned him his first Pulitzer nomination. Few suspected that Hutchinson had never graduated from—indeed, had barely attended—college.

Nonetheless, via an idiosyncratic route, he also became an academic. Late in the fifties, he applied for admission to the history program at Chico State but was turned down. Hector Lee, dean of the college, was aghast at that, so he referred Hutch to the English department where, in special recognition of his literary achievements, the author was admitted directly into the graduate program. Hutch took his lone degree, a Master of Arts emphasizing Western American Literature, in 1961.

In 1964, he was hired by the same history department that had refused to admit him as a student. The next year his magnum opus, a two-volume biography of Thomas O. Bard, *Oil, Land, and Politics,* narrowly missed a Pulitzer Prize but did win the Commonwealth Club Medal for Excellence and an Award of Merit from the American Association of State and Local History—not the first or last honors he reaped.

He soon became the department's—actually, the *school's*—leading character and best-known teacher. One ex-student remembers his introduction to Hutchinson: "The first day of class, the professor walked in wearing western work clothes and a Stetson, squinted at us, then growled, 'Somebody close that goddamn window. It's colder in here than Presbyterian charity.'" Recalls another, "He was a crusty old bastard, with sort of a whiskey-soaked air about him as he prowled the campus." No one ever played the role of Hutch better than Hutch; he was a virtuoso at it.

In fact, he was a virtuoso at many things: a devoted family man and a rigorous professional. An Old Grand-Dad liquor sign decorated one wall of his office, but not because Hutch was a dipsomaniac; no, he really was an old grand-dad to his students, loving but demanding. "He had this casual cowboy demeanor, but Hutch could lance bad ideas faster than anyone I knew," recalls yet another Chico State graduate. He certainly did something right, because in 1968 he was named Distinguished Teacher at Chico State. Nine years later, the trustees of the nineteen-campus California State University named him Outstanding Professor for the entire system.

In 1977, the Outstanding Professor delivered a revealing commencement address at Chico State, telling graduates:

151

I have asked you to read—much against your will—and I have asked you to write—against even stiffer resistance—and I have asked these things for good reason. You see, if you do not read, you cannot write; if you cannot write, you cannot think; if you cannot think, you cannot discipline your thoughts and if you cannot discipline your thoughts, you must forever remain fair game for every unisex charlatan with plunder in its heart. . . .

I have tried as well to bring to your attention what I came long since to regard as the fixed virtues of the human condition—truth, honor, valor and communion with God, fortitude and magnanimity. And I have tried, day in and day out, to suggest by actions, not mere words, that the true humanist is the one who *can* and *does* find joy in work, whatever that work may be.

Hutch taught and lived from a set of established values, and he could seem intransigent to soft thinkers. Actually, he was open to rigorous, well-documented arguments—I saw him reconsider positions many times. He certainly had his fair share of opponents. "You'd *better* have some," he commented. "Do you want the yahoos and nabobs to consider you their kind of guy? You have to worry about what's right, not about pleasing people." In fact, few folks seemed to be indifferent to him one way or another.

His scholarship was original, crisp, and unflinching: He insisted on the multiethnic heritage of this state's farming ("Agriculture: An Immigrant Saga"), revealed the California roots of the Paul Bunyan legend ("The Caesarean Delivery of Paul Bunyan"), rebutted the widely held "Octopus" stereotype of Southern Pacific Railroad ("Southern Pacific: Myth and Reality"), and generally attacked the power of the popular West-that-never-was ("Wilding the Tame West"). For Hutch, history was a process, not merely facts and figures.

Moreover, he also believed that we bear considerable responsibility to the future as well as the past, and that we cannot effectively shape the former without realistically understanding the latter. "This is clotted nonsense!" he might scrawl on a mushy thesis. He dismissed Peter Farb's best-selling *Man's Rise to Civilization* with a long, point-by-point rebuttal, one that concluded: "I would be remiss to my conscience if I did not try, which is all any mule can do, to persuade you that the 'reality' of the Indian story is quite adequate to wrack the conscience, without distortion, polemic and self-serving by popularizing authors."

The writer or editor of fifteen books himself, Hutch confirmed in volumes such as *California: Two Centuries of Man, Land, and Growth in the Golden State* (1969), *The World, the Work, and the West of W. H. D. Koerner* (1979), and *California: The Golden Shore by the Sundown Sea* (1980), as well as the aforementioned biographies of Rhodes and Bard, plus hundreds of essays and lectures, that he rated with Henry Nash Smith, Lawrence Clark Powell, and C. L. Sonnischen as one of his generation's most important scholars of western Americana. In 1985, he received what he considered perhaps the highest honor of all when he was elected a Fellow in the California Historical Society.

Despite those and many other honors regional and national, Hutch was as apt to be drinking beer and palavering with groundsmen and janitors as with Ph.D.'s. He refused to lose his common touch just because he had been gifted with an uncommon mind. "I learned a hell of a lot from guys like those before I ever got to college," he pointed out.

I had the opportunity to appear on a couple of public panels with Hutchinson. When Chico State opened its new library a decade ago, for instance, I joined Jacqueline Hall, Powell, and Hutchinson in a discussion of California and the West. Forty minutes into the performance, Hall whispered to me: "I love appearing with Hutch. I never have to worry about preparing because I never get to talk." When she told him that, he roared. No one was quicker to laugh at his own foibles.

In 1973, I edited a series of taped lectures on American literature and persuaded Hutch to record one. It opened this way:

> In opening this discussion of the cowboy in literature, it seems best to come down before the footlights even as Iago, boldly to proclaim my villainy. What follows is personal opinion, that same eflatus that sustains the editor in his aberrant judgment and causes the benighted poker player to draw three cards to an inside straight. This opinion has been formed over a lively lifetime, much of which has been spent reading western stories—first as an avocation, and then for vocational guidance.
>
> The difference is that between keeping a mistress and being married. In the first instance you read for entertainment, happily collaborating with the author to bring about the willing suspension of disbelief that is essential to the enjoyment of fiction. In the second case, you read to learn what other practitioners can tell you about grabbing the readers by the throat and giving it to them while their eyes bulge.

It was vintage Hutch. His vocabulary was voluminous and unlikely, his knowledge vast and diverse, his style playful.

Part of what made him so fascinating a friend, conversationalist, or adversary was the eclectic nature of his mind—he had done a great deal and read a great deal. He seemed well informed on nearly any subject—the water politics of the Sacramento or Euphrates river systems, the relative merits of cable tool and rotary drilling rigs, ethnicity in the Philippine Islands, Hispanic weavers of the Southwest—and he could tell you more than you ever wanted to know about it and make you enjoy it. This guy, who looked like he'd just wandered over from the bunkhouse, also managed to present an original angle on most issues. He was an unconventional thinker, not the least bit shy, who seemed to have swallowed a thesaurus.

It was easy for Chico residents to forget that old Hutch, as he was affectionately called there, was far more than a local character. As Lawrence Clark Powell summarized, "All I can say—and it says a lot—is that Hutch is to California what [J. Frank] Dobie was to Texas. Give us more men to match these two."

And Hector Lee, the noted writer, folklorist, and longtime chum of Hutch, recalls, "He kept friend and foe alike on their toes because he'd jab you in a second if you made a mistake. And he expected you to do the same to him. To Hutch, life was give and take and he could do both."

Most of all, though, he was a thoughtful, compassionate, absolutely trustworthy friend. I could call on him at any time for any reason. When one of our adolescents turned troublesome, he cooled my hot temper and predicted that firm patience would be rewarded; he was correct. When my father was slowly dying at our house, Hutch telephoned regularly to buck up my wife and me—despite his own infirmities and his wife's ill health.

The day before a heart attack felled him, he phoned and wished Jan a happy birthday, then asked, "Where's Dog's Body?" When I took the receiver, he was mumbling, "How such a lovely woman could have such poor taste in men . . ."

We palavered for a while about water politics in the Central Valley and how to save remaining riparian forests there and Hutch suggested research sources and some people I should call. Then he signed off with another of the lousy jokes he loved: "Did you hear about the fat lady riding her bicycle by the Catholic Church one Sunday who called out to a man she saw standing there, 'Is Mass out yet?' and the guy replied, 'No, but your back's showing.' "

155

While I laughed at his corn, he said, "So long, Dog's Body. Hasta la vista."

A couple of days later, Hector Lee called to let us know Hutch was dead. I told Jan, then we stood silently, holding one another. Hutch didn't leave footprints when he crossed the divide; no, he left boot prints, and I don't see anyone on the horizon who's going to fill them.

Bronzing the Valley

TWO SUMMERS ago I sat in McDonald's in Oildale drinking coffee and shooting the breeze with old neighbors, when one—a Dust Bowl migrant—announced, "The thang is, we're lettin' Mex'cans take over. You just wait," he warned, "we're all gonna have gingerbread grandkids. What're we gonna do?"

It's an ironic question. In 1846 Manuel Micheltorena, the last Mexican governor of California, declared, "We find our-

157

selves threatened by hordes of Yankee emigrants . . . . What are we to do?"

Since I am what my old neighbor might call a gingerbread grandkid—my grandmother's family migrated from Mexico— that false issue doesn't concern me.

Others do.

Despite early Spanish explorers, the Central Valley never had more than a faint population of Hispanics before the United States took control of it. Captain Pedro Fages's 1772 expedition is thought to be the first party of Spaniards to view this Valley. Skirting the eastern shoreline of San Francisco Bay, it was forced inland by Carquinez Straits. Eventually, the party climbed a spur of Mount Diablo and, to quote expedition member Fray Juan Crespi, "We ascended a pass to its highest point in order to make observations, and we saw that the land opened into a great plain as level as the palm of the hand . . . all level land as far as the eye could see."

Four years after Fages and Crespi first viewed the Valley, Padre Francisco Garcés entered the region's southern reaches while seeking a new route to Monterey from northwest Mexico. Crossing the Tehachapi Mountains, he came upon "a great river which made much noise and whose waters [were] crystalline, bountiful, and palatable." Unable to swim, he was carried across the Kern River's icy water by four Yokuts, whose village was near the present site of Bakersfield.

Although Spanish penetration of the northern Valley dated to journeys led by Francisco Eliza (1793) and José Antonio Sánchez (1811), and although Captain Luís Argüello guided parties into the northern Valley in 1817, 1820, and 1821 in search of possible mission sites and actually named the Feather River (*El Río de las Plumas*) in 1820, the region of the Sacramento nonetheless remained largely unexplored. The major Spanish explorer of the Valley was Gabriel Moraga, who between 1805 and 1817 led a number of excursions here and bestowed such names as Sacramento (sacrament) and Merced (mercy) rivers, plus Mariposa (butterfly), Calaveras (skulls), and, of course, San Joaquin and Tulare.

In truth, despite their early penetration and nominal control of the area, neither Spaniards nor Mexicans controlled the Valley. American trappers began traversing it with impunity in the late 1820s. It was considered a wild domain, a haven for fugitives and, for a while at least, a great source of potential, if unwilling, neophytes for coastal missions.

Hispanic settlement in Central California did not effectively extend beyond a narrow coastal strip. With all the advantages offered by coastal mission sites, there seemed little reason to extend settlement inland, although the Franciscans dispatched several parties into the Valley seeking possible new locations; a setting on the Kings River was given serious consideration.

Only a few sparsely populated Spanish and Mexican settlements developed in the interior: Pueblo de San Emedio south of Bakersfield is thought to be the oldest. East of Coalinga, on the site of an old Yokuts village, was another tiny community named Poso Chana. Another hamlet called Las Juntas developed near present-day Mendota. All three of those villages were populated in the main by AWOL Spanish or Mexican soldiers, plus their mestizo families. All three were small and isolated.

The contemporary political model of Hispanics being a colonized people doesn't work well in the Valley, but today the so-called Anglo majority is rapidly becoming a minority, and the so-called minority is itself becoming more Californian than Mexican, a reality some are loath to admit. The 1990 census revealed that in four San Joaquin Valley counties the population is already at least one-third Hispanic—many Central Americans are entering the mix—but only 10.8 percent of elected officials are, in local parlance, "Mexicans."

Mexican America is culturally complex and by no means unified within itself, because while other migrant groups have arrived in waves, then settled, the proximity of Mexico and the braiding of economies—theirs weak, ours strong—produce a constantly renewed first-generation of migrants, most from Mexico's least-advantaged, least-educated classes. Thus Latino society at any point may contain enormous variation.

Many new arrivals are sojourners who leave their families in Mexico, while others travel as families and try to take advantage of California's opportunity to escape perpetual peonage in their native land. The progeny of some retreat into Pendleton shirts, headbands, and a despairing sense of *carnalismo*; others move into the larger, mixed society; still others—including professionals—remain in the *barrio*, dedicated to elevating conditions there. Latinos are not as homogeneous as some activists wish or as some Anglos fear.

Eddie Lopez recently retired as book and travel editor of the *Fresno Bee*. He had been honored as this state's top Chicano journalist. Born in California, he is proud of his heritage and aware of its ambiguities; long before it was popular, he was up front about being of Mexican descent. He is also certain of his own accomplishments: "I hope my example will lead other kids into journalism, which means I hope they'll get a chance. You can influence the larger audience if you're willing to understand and communicate."

Lopez is a handsome man, his olive features haloed by steel-gray hair, and he pats his wife's pale hand—her parents were Okie migrants—as he smiles and says, "Look, I'm just a high school graduate, but I've worked my tail off and managed a satisfying career—a newspaperman for forty years. When I came up I didn't ask for any special breaks because there weren't any."

Dolores Huerta also speaks English, the language of power,

and does it well. Of course, she speaks Spanish too. Raised in Stockton, she has become one of this state's best-known Chicanas, a public spokesperson for the United Farm Workers, its first vice president, and a realist. "Don't be fooled," she warns, "it is still extremely difficult for nonwhites to escape poverty in this state, which means in this Valley. The odds remain against us."

It is sometimes surprising to realize that, despite the prominence of some local vaqueros and ranchers, there were no large numbers of Spanish or Mexicans in the Valley until the period between 1910 and 1930, when many workers from south of the border joined Filipinos to provide migratory labor in the fields. In 1931, as a result of their involvement in union agitation, and also because of the Great Depression, tens of thousands were repatriated, which left jobs open for the Dust Bowl migrants who soon entered the Valley in large numbers.

The next big influx of Mexicans occurred with development of the bracero program during the 1940s when World War II created an intense need for migrant workers. There has been a steady influx of both legal and undocumented Mexican migrants ever since, large numbers of whom return home annually. But a large and growing number choose to remain. As a result, many people of Mexican descent have moved into the middle class—some into the upper class as well—here in the Valley, and they have considerably enhanced what it means to be a Californian.

There is, however, no reason to become sanguine because political power reflecting the actual numbers of Hispanics has by no means been achieved. Is racism a factor? Absolutely— that and the genuine fear that attends it. Many Anglos have come to believe stereotypes that they originally invented. You don't have to travel far in the Valley to hear that a machine is so simple it is "Mexican-proof," or hear that the first words a Mexican baby says is "Attention K-Mart choppers," or that Mexico's national sport is knife-fighting.

The noted writer Arnold R. "Chief" Rojas, who worked as a vaquero in Kern County for many years and remained there after his literary career was launched, used to point out proudly that his ancestors were Yaquis and Mayos, as well as Sephardic Jews who came to the Americas to escape the Inquisition, a rich genetic stew indeed. He well understood the confusion of race and social class that has typified not only Mexico but also California. In what may be the most succinct observation ever made on the subject, Rojas explained in *Vaqueros and Buckaroos* the genesis of the "pure Castilian" Californios (a miraculous group when you consider how many years passed between what is called "*la conquista*" and the arrival of any numbers of Spanish women):

> The only way to acquire the land was to marry a daughter of the landowner. But they [the gringos] had already started a campaign of discrimination. They very neatly solved that problem by creating "Old Spanish Families" and marrying into them. But those who had no lands left became Mexicans, doomed to work for cheap wages and to suffer discrimination.

In this respect, little has changed in the Valley.

Although most Anglo growers and burghers publicly deny it, many tacitly agree that those who plant and pick and pack crops—and even the educated children of those people—are somehow not capable of governance. Wayne Flores of California State University, Fresno, explains, "Farm workers have been treated more like visitors than citizens."

There remains a strong hint of class prejudice here too. Within many communities, laborers—no matter what their color or their quality—have not been treated as equals. In fact, socioeconomic class hierarchies dictate that Anglos and Chicanos near the bottom of the barrel are least tolerant of one another and least apt to voluntarily mix, while those in the middle class frequently intermarry (over 40 percent of Chicano college graduates marry Anglos, and the number appears to be rising). This, in turn, leads some idealists to complain that it threatens the questionable premise that all Chicanos constitute "internal colonies," to quote John Chavez. Since in reality Chicanos don't constitute a homogeneous group, California—with the nation's largest and most diverse Latino population—renders such models only marginally valuable.

Some Mexican Americans—like many residents of communities in the prosperous Westland Water District—certainly do seem to be colonial captives, but the general pattern is that by the third generation in California, families of Mexican descent concede that education is the route out of poverty, and their youngsters pursue it. If those young people then intermarry, the blending that created *la Raza Cosmica* is further enriched in the Central Valley.

The population of Huron, the largest community in the Westlands Water District in Fresno County, is composed almost entirely of Hispanics who perform farm labor. The town has no junior high or secondary school. According to Don Villarejo, executive director of the California Institute for Rural Studies, 92 percent of the town's youngsters don't complete high school, so the cycle of agricultural peonage endures there. Growers are advantaged by this, but families trapped in poverty certainly are not. The per capita income in Huron, $5,501, is the fifth-lowest in the state. The four communities with still lower per capita figures—Orange Cove ($4,385), Parlier ($4,784), Mendota ($4,920), and San Joaquin ($5,356)—

are all also in Fresno County, and all have largely Hispanic populations. That county, of course, produces more agricultural riches than any other in the nation.

The principal reason that the population of those communities is overwhelmingly Hispanic is rooted in California's agricultural history. Corporate agribusiness in this state has always required large numbers of peons to work seasonally. Because many farm laborers manage to escape the cycle of seasonal employment, agribusiness interests find it advantageous to encourage a continuing northward stream of migrants who are desperate enough to accept any work they can find.

Most such migrants not only aren't citizens but also don't speak English. Moreover, many aren't particularly literate in Spanish. As a result, you don't have to contrast the composition of community governments with local populations to understand why Latinos are increasingly invoking the federal Voting Rights Act of 1965 to overturn the "at-large" voting system in favor of district elections that allow ethnic enclaves to elect one of their own.

When speaking privately to members of the traditional, pale-faced ruling elite in Valley towns, it is clear that they feel besieged by a people they do not understand, a people they have chosen not to understand. Most of their defiance stems from a sense that they are protecting their hard-won way of life from "foreigners." In this part of California, Anglos certainly do have as strong a claim to the territory as do Hispanics, but that does not justify exploitation. As the late César Chavez summed matters up, "Our sweat and blood have fallen on this land to make other men rich."

The wealth generated by the Valley's productive fields has by no means benefited everyone locally. The American education system, the Mexican family structure, and community traditions have frequently clashed. A prominent Chicana writer recently claimed that Chicanos in Texas are in better touch with their "true culture" than are Californians. That there is a "true culture" to be salvaged when heterogeneous people from the south merge with heterogeneous people from the north—this time cultures, like economies, braid—is as questionable as trying to equate regions as varied as Texas and California.

The most enduring strategy employed to control other Chicanos is to invoke guilt about the loss of an abstract "true culture." By those terms, nearly every American citizen should be deep in cultural remorse—true Germans and true Canadians and true Japanese. The actual dilemma isn't how to remain in the Mexican past, but how to shape the American future to include the best qualities of the old culture.

Latino society also has significant internal problems that are rarely addressed publicly. That lingering allegiance to Mexico and to *la Raza*—to abstract *ideas* of those things—for instance, seems increasingly to be an issue of socioeconomic class, ineffective education, and, in places like Huron, of a lack of opportunity. Those trapped near the bottom cling to their versions of old, certain, perhaps less-challenging values.

But there is more: While no Chicano intellectuals lay claim to the Valley on the basis of its slim Hispanic history, some do posit a mystical belief that their Indian heritage somehow entitles them to that place and, indeed, to all of California. This view requires a notion of pan-Indianism that is at best romantic, at worst self-serving, since native cultures were as diverse and contentious as the Europeans who conquered them, which was one reason the conquest was so easy. A few prominent Mexican-Americans, however, reject such facts. At the conclusion of an exhausting bargaining session between an Italian-American farmer and a representative of the United Farm Workers, for example, the grower asked, "What do you *really* want?"

165

Eyes blazing, the union representative responded, "We want our land back!"

Such beliefs are strong precisely because they are matters of faith, of *Chicanismo*, rather than reason: This *must* be true. Such beliefs, too, complicate the already difficult lives endured by many Latinos, and young gang members in Valley towns have mouthed somewhat garbled versions of *Chicanismo* as rationalizations for their activities.

I recently heard a Chicano educator suggest that the notion of overpopulation was an Anglo scheme to retain control of California. "We need more babies, not less. When there are 100 million of us, we'll rule this state," he asserted.

"Will it be worth ruling?" I asked, thinking that we would have only the *remains* of the state to rule, like the black mayors who now govern decayed cities.

Beneath all such complications lies the Valley's self-perpetuating tradition of racism. In the eyes of more than a few—and herein are sewn the seeds of tragedy—lack of opportunity has led to distrust of upward mobility, an association of success with rejecting one's cultural heritage. Poverty and ignorance therefore perpetuate themselves. There are those who demand exclusive allegiance to a home country that offered little opportunity to its poor. But total rejection and blind allegiance are not the only options.

The rationalization for claiming American opportunity as Mexican due is the often repeated argument, "We are poor in Mexico because of what the Yankees did to us," but that claim ignores historical reality. Certainly they are poor in part because of what the Yankees did, but they are also poor because of what Mexicans have done to themselves.

Writer Richard Rodriguez suggests, "Mexico will determine California. I look at the new generation in my own family; my nieces and nephews are truly Californians, some with Anglo surnames and some with Spanish surnames. The bloodline is incredibly mixed, and we are all Californians."

Fred Dominguez's family moved to this Valley before California was American. Like Rodriguez, his face reveals the Indian ancestry of which he is unabashedly proud. He is a postal employee in Bakersfield and is especially pleased to point out that his grandfather and his father were locally famous vaqueros. At the time of our visit, he and his wife, Rachel, were entertaining guests, family and friends, and there was much laughter as people of various colors mingled, everyone seeming to be at least somewhat bilingual.

Dominguez speaks fluent Spanish, of course, but English is the language of day-to-day communication at home and at work. "I have to talk English," he grinned, "or these Okies'll take over," and two fair-skinned men laughed. His style of rough ethnic joshing is common in the Valley, old prejudice acknowledged but converted to intimate kidding. But far too much old prejudice still thrives.

As is true of Rodriguez's family, Dominguez's grandchildren are dark-skinned and fair, dark-haired and fair, with surnames Hispanic and Anglo, and all are the blood kin of "Chico" Dominguez and Ramon Dominguez, fabled vaqueros. And all are Californians.

Journalist Tony Castro has suggested that "The Mexican-American in the Southwest today is like a Palestinian in the Middle East." Much of the Southwest—unlike the Central Valley—certainly was Spanish and Mexican territory, but 40 percent of educated Palestinians don't marry Israelis. Analogies based on a static view of a dynamic culture do little to clarify contemporary problems.

There are Hispanics of all colors and all social classes in this Valley. There are people called Mexicans whose great-great-grandparents were born here and others who arrived this morn-

167

ing; some, like me, the progeny of a vaquero and a seamstress, are so genetically intermingled that we are Hispanic by choice; I tell my Chicano buddies, "I am your grandchildren." That prospect doesn't necessarily comfort them, but they understand what I'm saying.

There are also displaced Mexicans in the Valley, here out of economic necessity, not preference. There are people here struggling with tangled tendrils of memory and history, while others are intent upon forgetting the past and pursuing their futures in this heterogeneous place. There are also countless variations between those extremes.

"Ray Gonzalez for State Senator," read a roadside sign near Bakersfield in 1990, and low in one corner, swirled with a marking pen, was a bit of graffiti: "Chacho de loma—con safos." This was *un grito del corazón*—a cry from the heart of the otherwise-anonymous Chacho—proclaiming pride in his heritage, pride in his barrio, pride in himself.

That proximity of Chacho's *carnalismo* and Gonzalez's *assimilación* symbolized well the cultural extremes of a dynamic, diverse, sometimes fragmented people, and there is no reason to assume that Chacho more nearly reflects an ideal of *la Raza* than does Gonzalez.

The Bakersfield Sound

A T A small cafe on Sundays in Bakersfield, a man named Bill Woods gathers with other musicians who came here during or just after the Dust Bowl migration. They strum guitars; a fiddle screeches and everyone laughs. Beer flows, old songs are sung, old dreams revived.

Bill Woods has never made it big in the music business, but he is one of its most important figures in this state. In the late forties and early fifties, he drove around town in a car with

169

"Bill Woods and His Orange Blossom Playboys" inscribed on its front doors. He proudly played what we called "Okie music."

What none of us could know then was that Woods was a herald. He augured the prominence in country music of what is now called the Bakersfield Sound. Before the Southern music Woods played could reach a wider audience, however, it was necessary to soften its image. Cousin Herb Henson accomplished that.

On afternoons in the late 1950s, my family, like many in Kern County, clustered around a small television set late on weekday afternoons—"Is it time yet?"—watching the screen swerve into moving grays and blacks. Finally, a soft-looking, grinning man wearing western clothes appeared. Seated at a piano, he lip-synched his own thin baritone voice singing his theme song—

Y'all come!
Y'all come!

Before his recorded voice ceased singing, Herb Henson would stand, approach the camera, then grin, "Howdy frey-unds and neighbors."

My mother, a fourth-generation Californian and never a fan of what she called hillbilly music, nonetheless watched this program daily ("He's such a friendly fellow. And with a nice family too"). We didn't, of course, realize that hokey Herb, with his Gene Autry wardrobe, was helping to turn that alien music into what was being called country and western—although it had precious little to do with the West. Henson was able to do that because he really did make us feel as though we were his "frey-unds and neighbors."

"And now," the chubby cousin announced, "we'll let our lovebirds, Fuzzy and Bonnie, start things off."

170

Fuzzy Owen, handsome, dark-haired, and slim, like a bit player in the film of *The Grapes of Wrath*, stood arm in arm with pretty Bonnie Owens, just a kid then but already the first of Buck Owens's wives and destined one day to be Mrs. Merle Haggard as well. Those two sang a version of some currently popular love song—no lip-synching this time.

Everything was performed by a youthful cast, some of whom would in later years become, if not stars, then established artists. That they were only slightly off-key in those days was miraculous, because this was small-town, small-time television, and the camera would regularly jolt when someone tripped, or absently pan beyond the set to reveal embarrassed men in jeans and T-shirts.

More frequently, the camera revealed that gang of enthusiastic musicians in the background. The band might include Woods, Billy Mize, who looked like a movie hero, Jelly Saunders, with a fiddle thrusting from his chin, husky guitarist Glen Campbell, or youthful Buck Owens, blond and lively. All looked as though they not only could fight their way out of trouble but had on more than one occasion—tough Okies.

Then Cousin Herb, who looked and sounded more like a country preacher than a fighter, announced, "We got a real treat for you folks now"—again too close to the camera, his face distorting like photos of the curvature of the Earth—"our guest star, the great . . . *Tommy Collins* . . . singin' one of his own songs, 'You Just Better Not Do That.'"

Handsome, grinning Tommy Collins appeared on-camera, waved, then began to sing. He was a treasure to us, a star we—correctly or incorrectly—considered local. On another afternoon the guests might be the wondrous guitarist Joe Maphis and his wife, Rose Lee, both in gaudy, sequined cowboy clothes. On yet another show, it might be the rowdy, talented Maddox Brothers and Rose performing their risqué hit "Sally

171

Let Her Bangs Hang Down." On still another, diminutive, mischievous Little Jimmy Dickens might sing one of his novelty songs like "Take an Old Cold 'Tater and Wait"—

> *Now taters never did taste good*
> *With chicken on the plate*
> *But I had to eat 'em just the same.*
> *That is why I look so bad*
> *And have these puny ways,*
> *Because I always had to take*
> *An old cold 'tater and wait.*

When the number ended, the host approached his diminutive guest, who seemed to be indulging in a private joke with the bandsmen. "Where you gonna be playin' at this weekend, Jimmy?" asked Herb.

Little Jimmy, his speaking voice high like a Munchkin's, grinned into the camera: "I'm gonna be at Blackboard with Terry Preston and the Termites . . ." his eyes twinkled, and he added with a wink into the camera, "and don't nobody bring me no taters, either!" Everyone laughed too much.

Once the interview was completed, Cousin Herb's face drooped like a basset hound's. "It's time for our hymn"—also pronounced with two syllables ("he-um")—"and this goes out to our shut-in frey-unds."

Young as I was, I nonetheless saw the paradox of all those musicians—whom I identified with chicken-wire screens in front of bandstands, with the flash of flying bottles and quick fists—suddenly becoming so reverent. Now all, even Little Jimmy, were crooning "That Old Rugged Cross," and my mother's eyes dampened, but I—ever the skeptic—strongly suspected that few congregations had heard any of those guys sing at a Sunday service.

A clear dichotomy existed in the Okie subculture that thrived in the San Joaquin Valley then, and we locals didn't require sociologists to explain it. Half a block from the house where I was raised squatted the Tejon Club, a whitewashed, unadorned beer bar and pool hall that hosted oil workers like my father—from Texas, from Oklahoma, from Arkansas and points South—from whose jukebox only hillbilly tunes blared. The alley in back had hosted more fights than Madison Square Garden.

Another half a block beyond, on a grassless, unpaved lot, stood the equally whitewashed and unadorned Assembly of God Church, where few Tejon Club habitués ever assembled, unless carried there in a coffin.

Those two institutions summarized the stereotype of southwestern migrants at that time: men to fundamentalist saloons, women to fundamentalist churches—enclaves of Southern culture for the homesick. Country music had roots in each, the profane and the sacred, the barroom ballad and the hymn, but honky-tonk dominated the music's initial image.

The music began its life in California during the 1930s. "It didn't get started here until the Dust Bowl [migration]," explains historian Richard Bailey. "The Okies brought it."

What Cousin Herb Henson and others like him—Jimmy Thomason, Eb Pilling, Mize, Owens, and eventually Woods himself—accomplished in the 1950s, was to soften that raw image of both the people and the sound—alien *others* to many —without sacrificing the music's uniqueness.

As it turned out, Bakersfield's musicians did not later succumb to the allure of overproduced "pop" sounds. Few could afford the banks of violins, woodwinds, or brass, the choruses and echo chambers, that would in the 1970s discredit Nashville. Instead, they remained with the music's traditional sound —"Hard Country," it is called—at the very time when many in

173

the South were moving away from it in a rapid, embarrassing scramble.

Country music here is still characterized by a rough edge. Sings Merle Haggard,

> *I don't have to wonder*
> *who she's had.*
> *No it's not love,*
> *but it's not bad.*

Time referred to Bakersfield music as "scruffier, less polished." We locals call it more honest, more *country*.

The enduring theme of these lyrics hasn't been mama or beer or trains, it has been the historic clash of rural Southern versus urban Northern values—yearning for a pastoral life. In the Central Valley, displaced Southerners have found reason to perpetuate that yearning.

To reach its present prominence, however, their music had to escape the limiting image of honky-tonks and enter popular culture as an anthem for working-class folks of all backgrounds who hankered for their versions of rural values. Once it ceased to be Okie music, or even country music, and began to be blue-collar music, it was on its way. That process began in Bakersfield during the 1950s, and television programs like Cousin Herb's and Jimmy Thomason's and Billy Mize's were the major avatars of change.

Through it all, Bill Woods has been here. "Ol' Bill's the gran'daddy," says Haggard. Woods and his music have remained unchanged: He's a honky-tonk man who plays honky-tonk music. And we've learned to love it.

Leon Patterson's
Short Season

D URING THE decade following World War II, the
southern end of the Great Central Valley produced
some extraordinary athletes—Bob Mathias, Billy Vukovich,
Leamon King, Sim Iness, Frank Gifford, Rafer Johnson,
among others. There were many reasons for this: The region
was full of recent migrants whose youngsters were making their
way into the school system, taking advantage of opportunities
their parents hadn't enjoyed. The work ethic was instilled in
these Depression babies early. At that time it was not uncom-

175

mon for even middle-class youngsters in the Valley then to earn their spending money in the fields or packing sheds, for their parents viewed work as something sacred.

No athlete outshone Taft High School's Leon Patterson, the first high-school boy to put a twelve-pound shot over sixty feet. Patterson exceeded that mark seven times in 1952. He was also the nation's leading discus thrower, a solid sprinter, and the only prep football player in the Valley to rank with the fabled Gifford.

In June 1951, following his junior year at Taft High—he had just won three gold medals in the state track and field championships—Leon took a routine physical examination for a summer job in the oil fields. The physician found albumin in his urine and diagnosed Bright's disease (glomerulonephritis), an incurable, virtually untreatable condition in those days before dialysis. Moreover, the doctor also discovered that Patterson had only one kidney.

Remembers his oldest brother, George, "If you met him, no one could conceive of this kid dying of a disease. He was too strong, too healthy . . . he looked like he could bend crowbars."

A coach took the young man to a specialist in the Bay Area, who confirmed the diagnosis and advised Leon to give up sports. Leon quit football; fifteen major colleges, including USC, Notre Dame, and UCLA, had been recruiting the six-foot, 190-pound running back. He continued to put the shot and throw the discus.

There was something else about him that none of us knew at the time: Although he appeared to be the apotheosis of the California dream—blond, tan, handsome—he was, in fact, the product of a California reality—poverty, toil, grit. The Patterson family had migrated from Arkansas and, like John Steinbeck's Joads, drifted west in search of opportunities during the late 1930s. Leon and his two brothers grew up working as migrant farm laborers, doing men's jobs when they were children. "Mom and Dad followed crop harvests," explains George Patterson. "They were basically field hands until we got to Taft. We all were."

Leon's impecunious parents put the boy to work when he was six years old, and he was soon an experienced laborer, unafraid of hard work—or much else, for that matter. He was not raised to expect life to be easy, because it wasn't. The demanding regimen of childhood labor did produce an exceptional physique.

The Patterson family had by then established itself in parched Derby Acres near Taft, on low desert hills about forty miles west of Bakersfield. Leon's father had found a job as a roustabout in what locals call the oil patch. Later he worked as a well-puller, then he became a marginally successful oil-field contractor, but as his oldest son, George, remembers, "Dad's drinking held him back all his life." In fact, alcoholism, the attendant poverty, and occasional drunken violence seem to have dominated the family's life.

"Leon had never had a steak, a lobster, or a salad in his life," reports Dixie Kinney, his high school sweetheart and wife. "I don't know if he'd ever had Christmas gifts, but he'd never had a Christmas tree," she adds.

There was more. "Not once did his parents come to any of his track meets," she reveals, "not even when he won state championships. When the town honored him with a banquet, they didn't attend."

Patterson struggled to become a good student. The cycle of migrant farm labor hadn't ever allowed him to settle in at a school, so his basic skills were thin. "Most of our dates were spent doing homework," Dixie explains. "Leon was a smart kid, but by the time he got to Taft High, with his parents moving from one crop-picking job to another, he'd been to forty-two grammar schools. He was never caught up in his schooling, so I helped him a lot." His education, however spotty, caused problems at home for Leon because, like many southwestern migrants, Marvin and Lillie Patterson were poorly educated and never entirely comfortable in California. Their youngest boy was becoming a Californian with a Californian's sense of the possible.

Following his graduation from high school, Leon accepted a full athletic scholarship at the University of Southern California, the grant extended by Trojan track coach Jess Mortenson even though he was aware of the gravity of Patterson's illness. Leon told him, "I hope God at least will spare me until the next Olympics."

God didn't, but if Leon had only thrown as far as he did in the spring of 1954, if he had not improved at all, he would have won a bronze medal in the 1956 Olympic Games. He was the real thing.

Leon and Dixie were wed in 1953 and lived in USC's married students' housing complex, an environment far removed from the farm-labor camps of his childhood. In 1954 they became parents when Leon Junior was born, but their joy was tempered when the young father's blood pressure began to soar and his extremities began to bloat as his lone kidney failed.

Nevertheless, Leon achieved perhaps his most remarkable athletic feat at the National Collegiate Athletic Association's championship in Ann Arbor, Michigan, that year. As teammate Dick Bank remembers, "His feet and ankles were swollen, affecting his ability to move quickly in the ring, and he was way behind in the [discus] competition, but on that last throw . . ." The smallest and certainly the least-healthy competitor, Patterson somehow managed to concentrate his remaining energy and whip the plate far enough to earn third place against the nation's best.

World-class athletes are, to paraphrase F. Scott Fitzgerald, different from you and me. In general, they don't like to lose at anything. Leon was no exception. His USC teammate, former national pole-vault champion Ron Morris, has never forgotten him: "The guy was a super athlete. . . . He was *really* competitive. We'd have crazy contests—who could throw a discus farthest while standing on one hand or who could walk the farthest on his hands or who could long-jump farthest backwards."

In the fall of 1954, Leon's vision failed because of high blood pressure, and he was taken to Good Samaritan Hospital. By then, none of his friends and family could fool themselves about Leon's prognosis, but neither did anyone anticipate how agonizing the course of the illness would be. Or at least no one but Trojan miler Jack Larsen, one of Leon's closest friends, whose father had earlier succumbed to Bright's disease. "The night before Leon died, I held his hand," he reveals. "There were four or five of us in the room, and I said, 'Leon, what can I do?' He said, 'My lips are dry, can you get me some water?' I wet a towel and put it on his lips. He was so bloated that his eyes were swollen shut. It was brutal."

It was indeed brutal. Leon's entire family—parents as well as wife, infant son, and brothers—were with him when his suffering finally ended. If his mother and father couldn't appreciate athletics, they did know the obligation of blood to blood and were there when he most needed them.

Well into middle age now, his teammates have never forgotten the remarkable boy who barely lived to be a man. Leon's grueling death was not scripted by Hollywood, and neither was his life. He was a real Californian who experienced real hardship, who enjoyed real triumphs, and who finally suffered a real death. Shortly before entering the hospital that last time, he attended the Trojans' football game against Texas Christian University, even though he was by then blind. He went to that game because USC, like Derby Acres and Taft, like the Valley and California itself, had become part of his expanded world. He had moved far beyond the rural Arkansas that had produced his parents.

Leon's life and death still haunt those of us in his generation. "We were just kids," Ron Morris reflects. "In the hospital he was upbeat, always talking about what to do when he got out. But he knew he wasn't going to make it, and we knew he knew."

At the 1952 state championship meet, true to the code of athletic modesty that ruled in those distant days, the ill athlete didn't strut or leap or jab his finger in the air after once more breaking the national record and winning another title. Instead, he grinned, accepted handshakes, and flashed an "okay" sign to Dixie up in the stands, his heavy shoulders sloping, his blond hair iridescent in the spring sunlight—the epitome of everything California was supposed to be.

Forty years later, he still seems to represent what was best in us. And not merely because he could throw a discus, put a shot, and run with a football.

Oildale

TO GAZE deep within myself, I walk the streets of Oildale. On December 23, 1985, frigid tule fog obscuring all but the nearest yards and houses, I wander up McCord Street—no sidewalks here, but many trailer parks in an area where once Dust Bowl migrants built hovels—and I notice two banty roosters scratching and jerking on a patch of brown Bermuda grass, eyeing one another but ignoring, as nearly as I can tell, two wild doves feeding with them. I stop and for a few moments stand motionless, watching while my breath bursts white, then one dove flies with a muffled whir and the other poses warily. Both roosters pause, fighters awaiting the bell.

With a hollow warble, the second dove climbs swiftly into the gray surrounding us, leaving me on the sandy border between lawn and street. I notice then two pickups parked on the far border of the Bermuda, one ancient and huge, the other new, small, and crowned with four yellow fog lights. On the older vehicle's blotched surface someone has painted "Trust Jesus." A bumper sticker on the new one says, "If you love something, set it free. If it returns, it is yours. If it doesn't, hunt it down and kill it." The smaller pickup is metallic red, as are the roosters.

The neighborhood through which I wander is called Riverview because before a dam was constructed in the mountains east of town, you could view the Kern River flowing through your kitchen during wet winters. It was once considered the least prosperous section in this unaffluent and unincorporated community. Today, although new housing developments sprout on Oildale's outskirts, many of the same unpainted shanties I used to see here as a kid in the 1940s remain erect and apparently unchanged—like tribal elders, reminders of our collective past. Two or three rickety lawn chairs—poor people's air conditioners—sit in front of many such residences, as do cars or trucks whose grandeur often contrasts sharply with the setting.

Such older houses are now bracketed by ubiquitous trailer parks and what realtors like to call "upgraded" houses. The former feature everything from modern mobile homes complete with metallic awnings and metallic porches, to geriatric travel trailers, faded and frayed. Most of the upgraded houses are carefully painted, with yards that may be tended by dark-skinned men from other communities; moreover, there seem to be more and more signs announcing security systems, indicating perhaps a siege mentality, the long shadow of hard times past.

Now contiguous with Bakersfield, Oildale grew north of the larger town during the early years of this century. Lawrence Clark Powell worked in the area in the early 1920s and even then, he tells me, "We learned to leave the Oildale guys alone, thank you." It was an enclave of oil-company camps, attracting a disproportionate number of males who did hard, physical labor, and pursued rough, masculine diversions. Except that agriculture and not petroleum was the principal lure, this was also the pattern for much of the San Joaquin Valley, where waves of migrants have been attracted since the 1870s not by gold nuggets or movie careers but by the availability of what can only be called toil: Chinese, Japanese, East Indians, Mexicans, Filipinos, blacks, plus many varieties of whites.

Despite their resulting heterogeneity, most agricultural towns have by no means been racially integrated but have at least hosted residents of varied colors, whereas the oil industry, unofficially but actually, did not welcome nonwhites. So towns like Taft, Coalinga, and Oildale developed racist reputations. In my youth there was even said to have been a sign—which no one ever saw but everyone talked about—on the outskirts of town: "Nigger, don't let the sun set on you here."

In any case, my hometown's renown as a rough section intensified following the so-called Dust Bowl migration of the 1930s, when large numbers of Southwesterners settled here. This is Merle Haggard's hometown; Buck Owens's Enterprises is a major local business. Today, fifty years after that migration began in earnest, and now boasting its own hospital, its own high school, its own civic organizations, Oildale is nonetheless spoken of by local liberals as a redneck enclave.

A close friend of mine, a Bakersfield boy who understands well what my hometown *means* locally, mentioned the other night that his therapist had suggested that Oildale is a crucible for fascism, which might simply mean that people here voted for Ronald Reagan, hyperbole being what it is. But my friend guessed that the three R's—racism and rowdiness and the right to bear arms—were troubling her, so he rattled the therapist's cage, telling her about the night a group of us, all high school pals, had driven to my house from Bakersfield. In our exaggerated sense of adventure, we suggested that the one black among us duck as we entered Oildale—he laughingly complied—then we dashed from the car into my place where we spent the night.

While our dramatics were unnecessary, they symbolize an aspect of Oildale's lingering reputation among those who do not live here. It is said to be an environment unconducive to notions as diverse as affirmative action, gun control, cigarette warnings, and seat belts. More to the point, Oildale has been to Bakersfield as Bakersfield has been to California, a scapegoat; "You're from *Oildale*?" I've heard at genteel parties, tone saying it all.

It is also what thin-wristed experts like to call a working-class area, and it remains predominantly white. Because so many of Oildale's citizens over the years have been fair-skinned Southwesterners, lovers of country music and the self-serving version of patriotism it posits, the community has been assigned a gothic Southern stereotype. This has been aided by the more important fact that many white migrants were poorly educated, products of generations of yeomanry, so they had to compete with nonwhites for jobs on nearby farms or work in the now-integrated oil fields. More than a little local pontification on matters racial has been in fact an expression of economic fear.

Racism, as well as other narrowness, hangs on most desperately among the desperate, but in this state it cannot be easily separated from issues of social class, for the latter, usually unspoken but as real and as certain as the surging of sex, often triggers racist regression. Here in California some nonwhites—the number need not be large, only visible—have been able to take advantage of the state's educational system to escape chronic destitution and assumed inferiority. While the society as a whole benefits from such a development, to whites stranded on that same desperate level, the underclass, even the slightest gain for nonwhites is clear evidence that something is wrong with America: *This is white country but a damn Mescan's bossin' me. Shee-it!* This is one reason why racist organizations tend to contain so many marginal members rather than men and women of accomplishment; the former are the threatened ones.

In the court of $225-a-month houses across the street from my folks' place, I see fair-skinned young men with long, unkempt hair, bearded, disheveled, angry after three beers at a world that does not offer them well-paid jobs or much prestige but does provide drug dealers to rip them off and does provide candy-bar and soda-pop lunches. They carry homemade tattoos on their knuckles, and their shoulders are splendid with murals of nude women on horses, but few high school diplomas grace their mantels: School sucks, man. If asked, they will often reveal that they are about to tell someone off or to kick someone's ass.

Christmas Eve, 1984: I walked out of my mother and father's small house and heard howls and screams from the courts. One young man was beating another in the street while two women shrieked and a third man yelled encouragement. The puncher was shouting over and over at the punchee something like "Take my fuckin' money!" It was not a new scene to me, but that night it struck me: Those cries should have echoed through the halls of Congress, or through that therapist's office, because they were battling each other in lieu of opponents they could neither see nor understand. And I, raised on this street, having seen my father fight here and having bled here myself, fresh from a comfortable Christmas celebration with my family, I knew exactly what was going on and was swept by imprecise guilt along with enormous gratitude for my own good fortune. But I did not allow myself to say, "There but for the grace of God go I," for I did indeed go there, or at least some part of me did. A moment later, a sheriff's cruiser pulled up and I returned to the warmth of family within my parents' house, reminded as my hometown frequently reminds me of the proximity and the possibility of poverty, and of its consequences.

Not only young men dwell in those $225-a-month units. My own grandmother lived in one—$50 a month then—and those small houses have long been refuges for the impecunious old. Many young women reside there too, more all the time it seems, often single mothers, also poorly educated and often tattooed—a small butterfly on a shoulder, a rose on one breast. In their too-young, too-fleeting primes they may combine bad teeth with bodies that make men gnaw chrome, but their boyfriends gnaw something else and soon babies ride on each hip; with them come food stamps, hours watching daytime television, and, usually, revolving males who cannot support themselves, let alone families; and with them may come the unfocused outrage that accompanies an erosion of hope.

As is true of people floundering at the bottom, these young and old, women and men, tend not to see over the rim to reality, so they remain frustrated by and angry at a world that offers them only blue-light specials. And when things go wrong, as they so persistently do, someone must be blamed: Mother dies and the damned doctors are responsible; the car doesn't run and the dirty Japs are guilty; I don't get the job because that other bastard has suck. Niggers cause this, and Jews, and slopes, but mostly niggers, because blaming blacks has long been an acceptable way for lower-class whites to vent general grievances. Anyway, Rambo or Jimmy Swaggart or the Klan will save us—white men banded together. And no niggers better move into Oildale because this is white people's territory; at least we're better than niggers. It is an irrational, probably unavoidable stance, one held with the desperate, uncritical grip of divine revelation: It *must* be true.

My own parents, for reasons I've never fully understood—his better education, probably, and her Latin attitudes—but for which I remain constantly grateful, did not indulge in such delusion. Instead, they taught me to accept people as individuals; my dad's dictum, for example, was "Is he a good guy?" not "Is he colored?" Thus Quincy Williams and Freddie Dominguez and John Takeuchi slept and ate at our house, just as did Raymie Meyer and Ernie Antongiovanni and Tommy Alexander. If my folks had given me only that I would have been well served.

Poverty and race and class churn a bitter stew. History dictates that a much larger proportion of blacks than whites inhabits the dungeon of unabating want, so race has been and remains an effective camouflage for our system's inability to reach many endemic poor. Because it is convenient to keep the hungry fighting one another, racism is frequently *part* of poverty, just as idealized egalitarianism is *part* of liberalism: default assumptions.

I must challenge my pal's therapist. Oildale is not a breeding ground for fascism, but poverty certainly is, poverty and ignorance and hopelessness so deep that education and government programs cannot deflect them. My hometown is a place where low-rent housing and the rumor of jobs for the unskilled have traditionally attracted whites on the bottom who hope to struggle toward the middle.

Those who do make that transition may carry lower-class fears and prejudices longer than is conscionable, but the real

187

problem is that others never make it. In Oildale you cannot be unaware of this nation's class system, because this is a cusp where hopelessness and hope, or at least the *hope* of hope, abut. When even that slimmest of threads frays, despair engulfs and violence erupts, in Oildale as elsewhere.

Therein lies the rub. Without this community and its un-pretentious styles, many people would be utterly abandoned by a society that fears fascism or attacks socialism but dreads and distrusts losers most of all, would be ignored by an elite often willing to love the poor only as it imagines them, not as they are: hopeless as well as hopeful. Since the poor exist, they must exist somewhere, and Oildale predictably harbors a proportionate number of losers: *Who's got the dope, man?*

But the losers constitute a small if visible minority here. I stride past the Assembly of God on Wilson Street, and from within I hear voices raised to a God who can accept, and I hear people—some of them from the courts, grown broad-hipped and repentant—praying for me, their brother burdened by sins unknown to them, but burdened, surely burdened, because that is the human condition and with God's help it can be endured. In that congregation now, as in the neighborhood, one might find a sprinkling of dark faces reflecting the slow erosion of stereotypes as well as the enduring truth that class profoundly influences the acceptance of nonwhites—too rich or too poor excluded. Unfortunately, the continued lack of blacks also illustrates the persistence of America's most heinous racist illusion.

What those who fear fascism forget is that most of Oildale is populated by folks who have established themselves in the middle class by dint of hard work, survivors whose daugh-ters now aim for honor roll and university, whose sons play football and fight wars. Oildale's citizens pay their taxes, fre-quently resent welfare, and shake their heads at punk rock, at

"Fit 'n' Forty" medallions, at sprout sandwiches, but accept the churning present anyway. When I stroll through town, nearly everyone I meet says hello, often with a southwestern drawl. Folks I've never seen before discuss the weather—"This *dern* fog . . ."—while waiting for traffic to pass. Their children have no drawls at all.

I notice other things on my visits home, little glimpses that I no longer take for granted. On North Chester Avenue, aging men and women who struggled here from Oklahoma now drink coffee in a McDonald's that is identical to several in Tulsa. There seems to be an inordinate number of Beware of Dog signs, especially on those blocks populated by folks who have edged into the middle class. And on winter mornings when fog doesn't obscure the world, steam plumes rise from the hills north, where, on the leases that lured so many here, leases where my father and I worked, heavy oil is liquefied by the hot vapor, then pumped to the surface.

It seems to me now that older women always boast hair care comparable to matrons in Palm Springs, their tresses freshly dyed, curled, piled, and sprayed. Coiffures are taken seriously even if bodies are not. The other morning, about 9 A.M., I passed a gal unlocking the front door of a beer bar, her hair deep red and swirled elaborately high above a leathery face imprinted "Texas, 1914." A cigarette dangled from her crimson lips when she smiled at me. I smiled back.

And there is an aggressive angle at which many men wear hats—billed caps, straw Stetsons, but no plaid snapbrims or berets—that advises you not to let your mouth overload your ass. Short sleeves may be rolled up, biceps bulging, and beer drinking after work seems sacramental. Cars and guns are icons taken seriously, offering reasons for taking oneself seriously.

It is finally the mix of people hereabouts that most compels. Friendly, plainspoken, conservative, Protestant in work ethic if not religion, scarred but not embittered by hard times, they constitute what I like to call a "front porch" society. In the days before air conditioners tamed the long, scorching summers, it was common for neighbors to gather on porches, drink iced tea, perhaps play cards or checkers, occasionally sing to the accompaniment of a guitar or banjo, but usually just talk. Many older folks still do these things, such gatherings livening balmy summer evenings, while kids clatter up and down sidewalks on skateboards now rather than skates.

Oildale is changing as the rest of California is, but its reputation is not altering apace. There is a sidewalk in front of my parents' place, built by the WPA in 1941, or so says the inscription on the corner. There is also a small parking strip there with a tree that has been so brutally trimmed that scar tissue knots it like tumors—a peculiar local style of arboreal coiffure that seems more ritual maiming than practical necessity. Below it, on summer mornings, runoff water from lawn irrigation settles in the gutter to make a small pond, and every morning if I arise early I can sip coffee with my dad and watch doves drinking out there—an unchanging reality—dipping their fawn heads, bobbing their white-splashed tails. They rise with a whir when a truck bounces past on its way to the oil fields. Then the birds return, drink again, and occasionally call—a haunting, hollow sound that says "home."

The Home

WAR IN the Persian Gulf was concluding. Northern California was at last being drenched by a storm. And in Petaluma my mother was dying.

Although wind and rain lashed the building, her rasping breath dominated the room. An opaque green tube delivered oxygen to her nostrils, another dripped fluid into a vein. I sat next to her, holding a hand no more responsive than clay; it was the only communication left for us. I kissed her immobile face,

191

but she did not react. This affectionate, this sensitive woman, who had once pumped life into me, was beyond my embrace.

But there is more. These events occurred not at my house, not in familiar surroundings as we had always planned, but in a convalescent hospital. I don't recall ever having declared that my parents would never end up in what Mom always referred to simply as a *home*, but I certainly believed that. I could not imagine circumstances that would so controvert everything I had ever learned about family and love and the obligation of blood to blood.

My mother's mother, her grandmother, and one of her uncles lived and died with us in their old age. Some years ago, when an aging neighbor broke her hip and was taken to a convalescent hospital, Mom was upset: "What a *terrible* thing to do. No one in our family was ever abandoned to a *home*." My Anglo father, not nearly as close to his own kin, nonetheless understood and acquiesced to the obligation inherent in his Hispanic wife's *familia*: You care for your own. You repay love with love.

But my mother died in a nursing home and I will live with that for the rest of my life.

Over half a century ago, Mom imbued not only a strong sense of familial duty in this only child but a passion for language, a passion for literature as well, and those things have shaped my life. She did this against the odds in my blue-collar family, speaking with me in two languages, reading to me in one, and bestowing on me affection that required no words.

Somehow, in a final bitter reality, all my hopes for her came apart. The spiral that undid them began when she suffered a stroke four years ago. She and my father had already purchased a mobile home in Petaluma near where my wife, five children, and I then lived. What I didn't know at the time was that my father, who avoided doctors, had already endured a series of occult strokes himself and was in the early throes of multi-infarct dementia and locomotor ataxia—meaning that his mental acuity and physical coordination were steadily eroding.

I moved them north, and Mom immediately underwent carotid artery surgery and stopped smoking. Despite desperately missing the neighborhood in Oildale where she'd lived for nearly fifty years, she seemed well on her way to recovery. My father suffered profound debilitation, so we moved him in with us and hired a nurse to care for him on weekdays.

Various of our children slept at Grandma's mobile home during that period, and I visited daily, but she was still alone too much. She had long suffered from agoraphobia, so she never visited any of her new neighbors, rarely left the confines of the residence she claimed to hate. Her behavior deteriorated—stalking her house all night, sleeping much of each day, dwelling on old grievances, old pain. Strange telephone calls from her became frequent, and nothing any of us could say or do seemed to help.

Her physician, at first baffled by this turn, eventually learned that Mom had undergone electro-convulsive therapy for intractable depression when I was a little boy, a secret even to me. That revelation—*shock treatments*—offered a clinical clue to her state, and a psychiatrist diagnosed her as suffering from deepening paranoid depression.

We had by then built a new house with rooms for my parents, so we immediately moved her in with us, a disaster for everyone . . . especially her, as it turned out. Mom was by then awake nearly all night, asleep nearly all day, reliving terrifying scenes from her past and constantly threatened by forces that only she could sense. Caught in a vortex of suffering that we could not relieve, she swerved out of control, and no balancing of drugs or sessions of therapy helped. This was not the old age for which any of us had planned or hoped.

Finally her local psychiatrist suggested that she be admitted to a psychiatric hospital, where she was stabilized and her sleep cycle returned to something like normal. During her stay there, I talked at length to a staff psychiatrist, telling her that I just hoped my mother could be made well enough to return home.

She did not immediately reply, and the pause alerted me that the problems were deeper than I understood. "Well," she finally said, "you have to be realistic. Your mother is fully incontinent, she's suffering from some dementia, and she's delusional. I think you'd better consider a skilled nursing facility . . . at least for the time being."

But I didn't want to.

I assembled the family and proposed that Mom move back to our house. We could hire another nurse, I reasoned, perhaps even twenty-four-hour help. The looks on everyone's faces told me how absurd my proposal was. My father by then could not walk and could barely feed himself; he required the constant care of a nurse . . . or of us. Pop had become, as they say, a load.

If you bring Grandma home, the consensus said, then Grandpa will have to be moved to a nursing facility. We can only do so much. Choosing between my mother and father was a decision for which I was unprepared, and it seemed to me to be unfair. It was also real.

My mother's persistent depressive behavior and angry outbursts—she slapped at least one nurse while living with us— added another element. Such episodes were terribly upsetting, especially to the children, who had previously known Grandma as a kind, doting lady. My sometimes rough father, on the other hand, became a pleasant, grateful patient, and everyone preferred that he remain with us. Mom's physician warned me: "Don't think mental illness isn't contagious."

Still I felt I *had* to bring her to our house for reasons that were themselves irrational—"No one in our family was ever abandoned to a *home.*"

Finally I had to relent. I visited the establishment recommended by both our family doctor and Mom's psychiatrist. That place haunted me. It was clean, and seemed both efficient and homey. It was also noisy—"Hellllp! Hellllp!" shrieked a woman's voice, and music echoed from an activity room. The head nurse accompanied me, and I saw people in various states of repair and disrepair, many strapped into wheelchairs. I was overwhelmed at the plight of so many elders—some drooling and dull, others lively and hopeful ("Hiya, Kiddo," winked one dapper gentleman)—all of them consigned to this strange nation of the old. One aged lady, who was pushing a wheelchair down a hallway, stopped me and begged, "Won't you *please* take me home?"

I departed shaken. My mother would *not* be condemned to a nursing home. By then it was clear that she would also not be able to live in our house, so I finally returned to the convalescent hospital for another inspection.

I talked with more staff members, and they seemed concerned and conscientious. The staff had a high percentage of registered nurses to nurse's aides. The head nurse explained to me with refreshing candor, "We sometimes have problems with aides. They're young, they're worked pretty hard and not paid awfully well, and some really aren't dedicated to the work, but we get rid of any who don't perform. If you're ever troubled by what a staff member does or doesn't do, let me know immediately. One way or another, I'll take care of it."

Her professionalism was comforting, as was that of nearly everyone I met that day, although I heard one harried young aide call in a dulcet tone, "How are we doing, sweetie?"; I found myself wondering how she addressed patients when visitors like me weren't present.

Despite assurances, I again left the nursing home overwhelmed by images of people strapped into wheelchairs like prisoners, gazing longingly at the door through which I so freely passed.

I telephoned our physician after that visit and said, "Tom, I can't leave her there. Isn't there a better option?" I explained what had bothered me, wanting him to tell me that I *must* bring my mother home.

"It's the nicest convalescent hospital in the area. Its medical facilities are excellent, and its training program for aides is the best. The place isn't the problem, Gerry, but the condition of the patients probably is. About 60 percent of them suffer from dementia of one kind or another. Most are there because they can't be cared for at home. Like your mother."

So there it was.

What followed fulfilled both my highest hopes and my deepest dreads. Many kind, concerned nurses and aides befriended Mom, but she remained agoraphobic; although fully ambulatory and not strapped into a wheelchair, she refused to participate in activities or to meet people in nearby rooms. "It's important that she not be in private quarters," I was advised by the head nurse. "In one of the larger rooms she'll have to interact with roommates." I had, naturally enough, wanted the best for Mom, and had asked about personal lodging for her.

Shortly after she began living in *the home*, she asked me if I remembered a movie called *The Snake Pit*. I said I did, however vaguely. "Well," she said with perfect cogency, "this place is a snake pit," and my soul swooped. As if on cue, that voice began shrieking down the hall, "Hellllp! Hellllp!"

Mom's sleep cycle reversed again, and when we next brought

her home to try living in our house—we did this twice more—
she called my name most of each night until I arose and found
her engulfed in dread that I could not alleviate. Indeed, I was
often part of it. My sleep was blasted, and I zombied my way to
work the following morning while she slept. Finally I returned
her to the *home,* my stomach a caldera of remorse.

Those experiments having failed, we moved her to a
residential-care facility, hoping the homelike atmosphere there
might offer a transition toward a return to our house, but that
experiment lasted only one raging night.

Mom's health slipped. I visited daily and began feeding her
when her vision failed. She ceased reading or even watching
television. Her world was closing. She still ate at our house at
least once a week, and often she would ask, "Oh, am I going
back to the *home?*"—that final word stabbing me.

As often, though, she'd insist on returning to her room at
the convalescent hospital: "Can't I go back to my room now?"

Much of the time she seemed to be herself again—a kind,
devoted grandmother who delighted in the various adventures
of her grandchildren and who was baffled by the professional
lives of my computer scientist wife and me. "You two're always
on the go," she remarked more than once. During those periods, I was certain she could return to our house, especially after
my father died last year.

But there were other episodes. Driving to my house for dinner one afternoon, she asked, "Who's taking the pictures?"

"Who's what?"

"These pictures, who's taking them? I never knew I'd be on
television." She was gazing out the car's front window.

Many times, as we returned to her room, she would ask, "Is
this the real room 15 or the other one?" The first time she asked
that, a long conversation ensued until it became clear that she
believed she lived in several rooms—all number 15.

And she continued stalking the halls at night, sometimes delusional, sometimes agitated, but as often friendly and co-operative—doing odd jobs the nurses found to keep her busy. Because she was bright and well-read and often humorous, she became one of their favorites . . . something of a character.

Days, if not awakened too early, Mom was warm, delighted to see family, and only slightly confused—"I must be nuts," she'd occasionally chuckle. She loved bananas and tacos, so I frequently brought her both. We'd chat, usually about my kids or her old chums—"Speck and I had *wonderful* friends," she'd smile. "We sure had fun." Yes, they did.

But we did those things in a nursing home, not at my house, and I was never completely free of the sense that I was letting her down. One afternoon an emaciated lady appeared in one of the beds in my mother's room. For several days I never heard her voice, never really saw her move, then one afternoon while Mom and I were chatting, I heard her call, "Harry . . . please come get me. Harry . . . please come for me."

I was engulfed by sorrow, for in that frail lady's call I heard the voice of all the others in the nursing home, of my mother, and of myself. Despite my suspicion that Harry would not be coming, I was nevertheless happy at least there had been a Harry. And that my mother too had known love. And that I had. In this life we can hope for little more.

It is easy, seductively so, to see these elders as merely old rather than as the sum of their lives, their intellects, their passions. Somehow that plaintive call, which I never heard again, reminded me of the layers of their lives.

With two-career families and electronic demands, the contemporary world is different from the one in which I grew up, but filial responsibility isn't. I acted considerably less than heroically through all this, and I sensed that I was digging a pit of guilt for myself, one from which I would never escape, yet I kept digging—cutting visits short, doing little to alleviate Mom's boredom, never as generous to her in her old age as she had been to me when I was young. Life seemed to be pulling in too many directions and I was weak.

While unable to escape the nagging sense that I was failing my mother, I found no alternative course of action. More to the point, part of me was relieved that I no longer had to deal with her from moment to moment, and of course increased guilt accompanied that relief as inexorably as death accompanies life; I could escape neither. Like those senior citizens who sat strapped in wheelchairs at Beverly Manor, I felt trapped. This situation was a reality for which I was unprepared, and my response to it was decidedly imperfect.

In one sense, everything ended in Beverly Manor on that stormy night last March. At least my mother's life did. But our connection remains intact and so does the haunting conviction that I could have, should have, done more.

I also understand that this pain is the price of love. If I hadn't cared then, I wouldn't care now.

Visions of the Valley

THE FAMILIAR vista of the Sacramento Valley from an airplane reveals more than a physical contrast: Obvious are roads, canals and fence lines slashing below, straight and measured geometry assignments. Equally obvious is the lurching course of a great river, feeder streams squiggling into it like a mad artist's doodlings.

Less obvious when viewing those features from above is that they represent opposing visions of the place. The canals, the roads, the fence lines are proprietary, profane reflections of

200

contemporary American beliefs; the streams are familiar and sacred reflections of Native American assumptions.

In what sense profane? The Valley was not the ancestral home of Europeans; they had no enduring link to it, so it was in no way sacrosanct. Moreover, they assumed theologically that nature was somehow the enemy of people—a beast to be domesticated, bought, and sold. Minds layered by generations of experience elsewhere could not accept this place as it was; as Francis Bacon long ago wrote, "We must bend nature to our will."

In what sense sacred? Indigenous cultures discovered their own existence in this Valley, the setting of their deepest memories. Here they grew in union with the environment; here they acknowledged questions beyond rational explanation; here they once sang, "*All my life, I have been seeking . . . seeking.*" The north Valley's native inhabitants, the Wintun and the Maidu, simply accepted the pulsing of the mighty stream. In the old days, the Sacramento River surged over its banks each spring, altering its course as it inundated the surrounding plain, depositing the rich alluvial soil upon which agriculture would be built. That intimate relationship between what they called the Plains of the World and Mother River was accepted by the Wintun and the Maidu. What are to us geographic features were to them eternal entities that had to be accounted for theologically.

As cited in Robert Pearsall's *The Californians: Writings of their Past and Present*, the Maidu described the birth of the river—literally their lifeline—this way:

A great surge of water came down and turned the valley into an ocean. Almost everyone drowned. Only two people got away to the Sierra.

Great Man blessed those Maidu with many children and all the tribes arose. One great chief arose among them and he traveled to the western mountains, but he found the valley still full of water. He stayed there for nine days without food or water, thinking about the plains of the world.

Thinking and fasting changed him. He was not like a man. No arrow could hurt him. He could not be killed. He called out to Great Man and ordered him to get rid of the water. Great Man tore open the Coast Range and made the water flow down to the ocean. This is how the Sacramento River was born.

The modification—mutilation, some say—of Great Man's work was accomplished as a result of another epic vision. The prophet was Robert Bradford Marshall, and he dreamed of rivers moved to regions where nature had not had the good grace to place them.

During the last decade of the nineteenth century and the first two of the twentieth, Marshall worked out a plan for taming rivers and remaking the Valley. His 1919 pamphlet, *Irrigation of Twelve Million Acres in the Valley of California*, contained a scheme remarkably like what has followed in the Central Valley Project and the California Water Project, right down to Shasta Dam in the north and A. D. Edmonston Pumping Station to the south—the elaborate complex of stored and transferred water that is at the core not only of Valley agriculture but of much economic and political power as well.

Over the last half century, a complicated series of dams and channels and strategically placed pumps has salvaged flow from mountain snowpacks. The Central Valley Project, a federal endeavor that delivers an astounding 8 million acre-feet annually, is considered the most ambitious public works project ever built. It includes not only Shasta Dam, its core, but also eighteen reservoirs, fifteen pumping plants, five power-generating complexes, and 540 miles of aqueduct. "The golden faucet,"

as historian Donald Worster calls it, eventually irrigated three
million new acres of privately owned land, a bonanza far greater
than the Gold Rush, and it can be credited largely to Marshall's
vision.

What is not much discussed or understood is that the difference between an image controlled by the river and a river controlled by an image bespeaks a cultural gap that contemporary
Californians have trouble grasping.

The Wintun and the Maidu considered themselves to be
part of the Valley, products of the same life force that created
the Earth, the sky, and, of course, the rivers. Another writer,
Frank Waters, explains that Indians believe "the emergence of
consciousness does not set man entirely free. He is still under
obligation to the dictates of the unconscious which embodies
all his primordial past."

This link to the primordial, to the mysterious nonrational, is
at the core of their sacred worldview. The Yokuts, who dominated the southern end of the Valley, chanted,

My words are tied in one
With the great mountains,
With the great rocks,
With the great trees,
In one with my body
And my heart.
Do you all help me
With supernatural power
And you, day,
And you, night!
All of you see me
One with this world!

For them, the Earth simply *was*; for Marshall and his society,

203

the world was what it could be . . . for a while at least. The two were nearly opposing visions.

Today, the traces of Valley Indians have been brushed away like an outlaw's trail; they are largely unrecognized in what was their home. Most of us have no sense of the people who dwelled in this great trough before European and American settlement, no grasp of their minds. In their place are visions nurtured in distant lands: Asia, Africa, Europe.

Burdened by neither European yearning for greenery nor overpopulation, native cultures of the great valley found it abundant indeed. Whether Wintun, Maidu, Miwok, or Yokuts, their mythology recounted no famines, although drought was not unknown. Like the mixed society that has followed them, they tended to build communities on watercourses, oasis settlements.

We newcomers, some of us at least, have retained the anachronistic attitude that we brought in the last century, a gluttonous confrontation with nature: big trucks, big hats, big talk— "We must bend nature to our will." It's our land; we *bought* it. We can do anything we like with it. We can pitchfork a salmon when we want, shoot a hawk when we want, dump chemicals where we want because the land is *ours*. In a time of dramatically diminished resources, illusions of inexhaustibility are obscene.

Often those illusions are linked to another historically fallacious attitude: Whoever is on the land has special rights to exploit it—mere presence guaranteeing privilege. One of my friends drifted north into Oregon and immediately began complaining about "outsiders" who were restricting logging. His presence, he insisted, should give him the prerogative to ignore any concept of the larger good. By that standard of thinking, there would be no Yosemite Park, no Yellowstone Park, no Sequoia Park; and, of course, there *is* no Tulare Lake anymore—the largest body of fresh water west of the Mississippi has been dried and plowed and planted.

There may soon be fewer open tracts to accommodate frontier gluttony. The recently signed Western Water Bill suggests that present Valley dwellers may endure changes as radical as Indians once did. Many growers, spoiled by past advantages, have convinced themselves that they are being abused; they threaten that if subsidized irrigation is denied them, they'll punish the larger society by no longer providing cheap food. They may, in fact, have to stop growing some crops—cotton, alfalfa, and pasturage for beef, for instance—that require excessive water. Garrison Sposito of the University of California at Berkeley, points out that those three crops alone use enough water annually to slake the thirst of 30 million people. If overpopulation continues, the Valley's next major harvest may be stucco houses on small lots.

Could it be that the agricultural vision that overwhelmed the sacred vision may in the next century find itself overwhelmed by an urban and suburban vision? Since 1964, seven million acres of this state's farmland have been lost to housing. A proposed light-rail system running parallel to Highway 99, plus Amtrak's expanding service, makes the vision of the Valley as a vast suburb at least plausible. Sposito warns that a Valley population of *sixty million*—ten times the present figure—is conceivable in the next century.

Remember, these figures are for a region that naturally endures an inversion layer—cooler air settling in the trough, trapped by warmer air above—so it has always been hazy. Now inversion traps pollution from industry, from agribusiness, and from cars, producing smog. The southern end of the Valley already suffers some of the worst air quality in the state, and scientists have demonstrated resulting health problems for people as well as reduced yield for farms.

205

Another vision is possible, if less plausible, given the press of expanding population and the profit motive. Thanks to the efforts of groups such as the Nature Conservancy, Ducks Unlimited, and the Sierra Club, plus various local organizations and state agencies, parts of the Valley are being restored. Native oaks are again being cultivated where once they stood, native bunchgrasses are being replanted, riverine forests and marshes and prairies are being restored. Could some version of the natural Valley be recreated? What seems most likely is a combination—diminished crops and expanding suburbs surrounding greenbelts of restored, protected flora and fauna.

Change is nothing new here. In the 1950s I worked part-time on a farm southeast of Bakersfield. Pulling a gangplow over a field then, I would occasionally feel a jolt and have to stop the big yellow Caterpillar. Often I'd find a granite mortar hollowed by a stone pestle that brown hands had once used to grind acorns.

From that tractor, I could gaze north toward Bakersfield, scanning a gridwork of fields in various stages of productivity. It seemed to me to be the hottest, driest place in the world, and I'd never have guessed that I was plowing the bed of what had been an eight-thousand-acre pond.

The south shore of what was called Kern Lake had also been the site of a prosperous Yokut village—thus those mortars and pestles. This setting, one that Americans had to "reclaim," had been considered abundant indeed by local natives; it gave them fish, waterfowl, antelope, and elk, among other game; it gave them tules for boats and shelters, hides for clothing and implements, jimsonweed for rituals. They lived on the land so they lived with it.

Another vision prevailed, and developers bent nature to their wills. They dreamt dry land where a lake was being reaped by Yokuts, and soon it was a field. They dreamt alien crops growing where native bunchgrass flourished, and soon the crops grew. They dreamt cattle where pronghorns and tule elk grazed, and soon the native ruminants were eliminated. Now many owners of the lake bed dwell in distant cities and send others—often brown people—to farm for them; they have no personal link with the land. The Yokuts' chant—*"All of you see me, one with this world"*—is faint as yesterday's wind.

What has been established over the past 140 years is the most productive unnatural landscape in the history of the world: chemically dependent agriculture. Writer Charles Bowden argues, "nothing done by Americans is for keeps—farms, cities, towns, mines, everything—constitutes a brief raid on the dry land and then becomes a tumbleweed. . . ." If true, what will be left in this valley? Many people fed. Selective wealth. Devastated water table. Sterilized, dusty soil. Teeming cities. Broken hearts.

Cattle ranching is the second most profitable agricultural pursuit in the state, but already, just a few miles west of the carcass of Kern Lake, at one of California's fabled ranches, San Emidio, that urban dream is once more about to be realized. The Kern County Board of Supervisors has approved a new community for 60,000 residents in a region that already endures abysmal air quality. This is prime ranchland, but it is expendable as the new vision of the Valley takes hold.

Jack Hunt, president of the Tejon Ranch Company, owner of San Emidio, explains, "We are managing the asset for the long haul only." No longer is this the Maidus' Plains of the World or the open rangeland of the vaqueros, or even the promising farmland that energized Robert Bradford Marshall.

It is "the asset."

What is next remains to be seen.

Other Californians

I T IS NOT a tourist's dream, the daylight journey from San Francisco to Los Angeles down the southwestern edge of the Great Central Valley. Brown hills press from the west, while irrigation rows seeming to flip by like fanned cards pull the eye toward the east, where the San Joaquin Plain stretches. Across it trees and plants sprout in geometric patches, but few people can be seen. This valley is vast, so from Interstate 5 extending eastward into haze toward the unseen Sierra Nevada there is a breathless sense of space: no houses, few trees, frantic whirlwinds dancing across an unplanted tract. Ahead the road shimmers as though flooded.

Night is more revealing and drivers are startled by a multi-colored galaxy of lights to the east that seems to extend, in differing densities, hundreds of miles along a plain once dark and forbidding. In fact, the Central Valley boasts nearly 6 million residents, as well as the fastest rate of population growth in the state. Those lights cluster mostly along the old route, Highway 99, for it is there that cities and towns have burgeoned: Bakersfield, Fresno, Stockton, Sacramento, and Redding; McFarland, Manteca, Live Oak, and Los Molinos. The nearby expanse remains void of lights due to corporate ownership: few small family-owned farms here, few communities, just land being tilled.

It is significant that those distant lights are multicolored, because so are the cities and towns and small farms. This Valley is the richest multiethnic rural environment in the nation. Even natives are sometimes unaware of that fact because the Valley's class system and de facto segregation disguise it. There has been a literal right and wrong side of the tracks here, with the affluent—mostly white—traditionally living east of the rail line and Highway 99 in neighborhoods with lawns and sidewalks; the less affluent often residing to the west. Symbolically, the highway has loomed like a local version of the Berlin Wall.

The principal reason for ethnic diversity in the Valley has been the availability of seasonal labor in agriculture, a constant here since the 1870s. People of all backgrounds have performed field work and have, in turn, themselves been viewed by growers as an indispensable resource. That reality has formed the basis of much of this rural society's social churning. An editorial appearing in the *San Francisco Morning Chronicle* on September 5, 1875, said in part, "The farm labor problem of California is undoubtedly the worst in the United States. It is

209

bad for the farmers themselves, and worse, if possible, for those whom they employ. In many respects, it is even worse than old-time slavery."

Because this has long been a place to start at the bottom—and, for some, to remain there—many seeking a foothold in American society have migrated here. A recent study revealed more than ninety distinct ethnic groups in present-day Sacramento alone. There have developed many ethnic enclaves in the Valley, towns with large concentrations of this group or that: Chinese in Locke, Basques in Bakersfield, Sikhs in Marysville, Swedes in Kingsburg. Woodville was originally called Irishtown because it was settled by a group from Northern Ireland. A Portuguese colony formed near Hanford, and another one developed in the Delta. Alabama Colony outside Madera was settled by white migrants from the Old South. Allensworth, a community of blacks in Tulare County, was founded in 1908 by an ex-slave, Lieutenant Colonel Allen Allensworth; it is now a state historical park.

Today there is a new, unofficial colony in the Valley, among the largest ever established here: 25,000 Hmongs, members of one of Southeast Asia's major groups, have settled in the region between Fresno and Merced. The Hmongs have faced resistance both passive and active from the sons and daughters of earlier migrants, who find them strange, as Okies and Japanese and Russians were once considered strange. These newcomers from Asia actually fit the Valley's pattern: "What brings the Hmong to Fresno is a peculiar vision," explains Frank Viviano, "composed equally of hope for a better tomorrow and nostalgic longing for the lost agricultural past"—shades of John Steinbeck's Joads.

"Foreigners," which usually means newcomers, have provided far more than labor here. An immigrant from China shipped the first load of potatoes from this region. The Chi-

210

nese, in fact, have contributed at virtually every level to Valley farming, and they have not been alone. Crops such as dwarf milo maize from Japan, alfalfa from Chile, and flax from India have been brought by migrants, and at least twenty different nationalities have contributed to the wine industry. As historian Anne Loftis has written, the Valley became "a laboratory of races," where groups often brought and practiced agricultural skills honed in their native lands.

For some, of course, their native land was here, the Valley itself, which once boasted one of the richest concentrations of American Indians on the continent—over 100,000, according to most estimates. "Three hundred tribelets of California's five hundred or more belong to this area," write anthropologists Theodora Kroeber and Robert F. Heizer. "Here were to be found most of her Indians, the predominant physical type, and carriers of the most idiosyncratic culture."

Today the Wintun, Maidu, Miwok and Yokuts remain the Valley's least-acknowledged ethnic groups—the long shadow of nineteenth-century abuses still seeming to hide them from those who usurped their land. They, who provided the state's first agricultural labor force, now tend to dwell on rancherias along the dominant society's edges, consigned to poverty.

Stereotypically confused with Mexican nationals (many of whom are themselves Indians), disguised by Spanish surnames, or assimilated by intermarriage, California Indians remain hidden in this their own land. But there is something deeper and darker at the core of the invisibility of this state's natives, some festering from the American past that extends far beyond the Valley's boundaries. Indifference, especially studied indifference, may be the greatest evil of all.

Ironically, East Indians have been more prominent in Valley agriculture than have American Indians. Enduring taunts of "raghead" from local nativists when they originally migrated

211

from the Punjab in 1905, East Indians turned out to be experts in irrigation, a skill vital to local agriculture. The Yuba City–Marysville area today boasts the largest concentration of Sikhs in the United States, more than 10,000, with new migrants arriving each day. It is a cultural center complete with a large temple, and Dadar Singh Bains, a local farmer, has become America's biggest grower of cling peaches. "The Hindu," proclaimed a commissioner of the state Bureau of Labor Statistics early in this century, "is the most undesirable immigrant in the state . . . unfit for association with American people." Today, "the Hindus" *are* American people.

The pejorative use of terms like "Raghead" and "Hindu," or "Slope" and "Gook" for Hmongs, is unfortunately also an old Valley tradition. Even more common has been scorn with which the term "Mexican" has been uttered by some, conjuring up images of stoop labor, knife fights, the ubiquitous, dark *them*. A ruddy-faced field foreman near Edison points toward a crew slowly working its way through a field that shimmers in heat and says, "Hell, they don't feel it the way a white guy does." The term "Okie" was for years a fighting word unless uttered with something close to reverence. Now, with the progeny of southwestern migrants well established, it—like "Spic" and "Hindu," "Wop" and "Portugee"—may be used with perverse pride by the grandchildren of early migrants, nativists and racists be damned.

Nativists and racists—especially those who, paradoxically, are themselves newcomers—consistently ignore the historical importance of immigrant cultures in the Valley. The San Joaquin Valley's most famous grower has arguably been Sicilian-born Joseph DiGiorgio. Coming west in 1915 with money earned wholesaling fruit on the East Coast, he had the capital necessary to dig deeper wells and pump groundwater from aquifers unavailable to those less wealthy. DiGiorgio also discovered that figs and grapes thrived near Arvin in the Valley's southern end. He acquired some 20,000 acres there and took advantage of modern techniques to improve his harvest. Eventually his holdings included some thirty farm properties in California, a dozen packing sheds, the Klamath Lumber and Box Company, three wineries, fruit auction houses in major eastern cities, plus ownership of the Baltimore Fruit Exchange—the list could be much longer—a considerable "farm" even by Californian standards. The *San Francisco Chronicle* once said, "DiGiorgio is to farming what Tiffany's is to jewelry."

And DiGiorgio was only one of a host of prominent Italo-American citizens in the Valley, citizens who, despite their accomplishments, remained "Wops" to some neighbors. Ernest and Julio Gallo became and remain the most productive wine producers in the nation, although they were challenged by Louis Petri. The Giumarra family of Kern County has dominated table grapes, and the influence of Michael Fontana's California Fruit Packing Corporation, the famous Del Monte label, has been profound. Although he did not live here, A. P. Giannini exerted great influence in the Valley through branches of his San Francisco–based Bank of America. Seeing the prominent positions achieved by many Italo-Americans, it is easy to forget that most of their families entered this Valley as laborers, that they too toiled and suffered under that faded sky, that they too faced discrimination. Like others who have succeeded, American Italians did so by dint of hard work, determination, and sharpness; nothing was given them.

Without "Wops," the Valley would be a different and a lesser place. Racial epithets are still employed by some people who know better, yet retain the habit; others, unaccomplished mostly, suffering poverty of mind if not poverty of means, still take solace in hoary illusions of racial superiority. Rough edges remain when varied cultures come together, especially when they are fighting one another for survival near the bottom of the barrel. Racism has been a problem hereabouts, though not an overwhelming one, and it emerges from a situation that also offers one of the region's great potentials: people recognizing shared goals and learning to live together in a class system that borders on a caste system. Intermarriages are increasing as commonality of experience and fate obviates ancient taboos.

Class looms larger than ethnicity in this Valley dominated by huge corporate agribusinesses. The same system that has produced such abundant farm yields has other consequences. The established model of ownership—vast tracts of land concentrated in the hands of a few—plus the need for seasonal labor, have social effects that are far from abstract.

Society here might be divided arbitrarily into five classes: the nonresident rich, corporate owners and executives; the resident rich, a group that includes family farmers, corporate managers, and successful professionals, along with those owning firms that serve agribusiness; a complicated and increasingly multiethnic middle class that includes many owners of small farms, many professionals, as well as those wearing both blue and white collars and providing services to the wealthy and impecunious alike; the upwardly mobile poor, some of them small farmers too, but most providing blue-collar work and frequently in the process of escaping the cycle of migrant labor; and finally, a considerable underclass composed in large measure of recent arrivals, along with those who have never managed to escape poverty's grip. In general, each level is larger than the one above it, and less white.

Of late, sadly, a new social class seems to be emerging—the downwardly mobile. Many people who have struggled to gain a foothold in the working class or the middle class now find themselves slipping back—losing their homes, losing their jobs, losing even their self-respect. They are as much victims of

214

the social and economic history of the Valley as of contemporary events, victims of the fierce struggle for what little wealth remains after the economic elite slices the pie.

There remains a dramatic and visible gap between haves and have nots in this region where, as historian W. H. Hutchinson points out, the annual value of crops exceeds the total value of all gold mined in the Golden State since 1848. Ostentatious wealth is not uncommon, nor is horrid poverty, and those things too mingle ethnicity and class: Explains political scientist George Zaninovich, the son of Slavic immigrants who farmed near Delano, "Wealth is viewed as racial, the proper domain of whites."

In 1980 the *New York Times* announced that six of the ten metropolitan regions with the highest percentage of population on public assistance in the entire nation were located in the Central Valley. The five poorest towns in California, according to the 1990 census, were located in Fresno County, among the nation's richest. It is true that nonresident poor come here seeking work, but it is also true that the economic system here has required that some people remain hungry enough to accept tough work in the fields. Labor, like land and sunlight and water, has been viewed as an inexpensive natural resource by growers in the Valley. Some people raised here since World War II have come to equate field labor with Mexicans—they *were* that inexpensive resource until Larry Itliong and the late César Chavez, the latter still a favorite target of local agribusiness, upset the system by organizing the United Farm Workers.

In this place that neither Spain nor Mexico ever effectively settled or controlled, the so-called Anglo majority is now becoming a minority, and Spanish is the second language. Mexican America is, of course, culturally complex because, while other migrant groups have tended to arrive in waves, and settle, the proximity of Mexico and the fluidity of shared history com-

215

bine to produce a constantly renewed first generation of migrants from below the border.

Dolores Huerta was raised in Stockton. She has become, arguably, this state's best known Chicana, first vice president of the United Farm Workers and the union's fiery spokesperson. "The pattern here has been *not* to recognize and acknowledge the contributions of nonwhites, like the Chinese who drained the Delta, for example, or the Blacks who contributed so much to cotton culture," she asserts.

There was no large population of Hispanics in the Valley until the period between 1910 and 1930, when large numbers of Mexican *campesinos* joined Filipinos in the farm labor force here. Today there are Mexicans of all colors residing in the Valley, a few whose great-grandparents were born here and others who arrived this morning. Many Americans of Mexican descent have moved into the middle class and above, but many more have not. Some are well-educated professionals, while others have never escaped poverty's icy grasp, and still others—frustrated by Mexico's lack of opportunity—are on their way here right now.

Says Manuel Alderette, whose grandparents migrated north in the 1920s, "The hard thing is to decide you're going to play by American rules. If you don't—if you avoid learning English and formal education and pretend you're still in Mexico, you might as well go back because you're going to be poor forever. I guess it's natural to want the best of both worlds: the old, familiar culture and America's wealth. But the most you can really hope for is what's happening here. In this Valley, there's a kind of compromise, a lot of Anglo culture but more and more Mexican too."

Khatchik "Archie" Minasian was raised in Fresno County, and he started life working in agriculture, "picking grapes, turning grapes, making boxes, doing all kinds of menial labor long hours into the heat. This is what life was in the Valley for most of the Armenians—in fact, for most of the people who were willing to work."

Fresno received its first Armenian immigrants in 1885 and today is considered one of the world's most populous Armenian cities, for they settled on their own terms and have contributed mightily to the community as it now exists. "The Armenians, who were a proud people," points out historian Loftis, "had the temerity to ignore the suggestions that they were not the equals of their American-born neighbors. They were competitive in business affairs and refused to be segregated to a special neighborhood."

One anonymous Fresnan was quoted as saying during the early period of Armenian settlement, "They are the only foreigners . . . who think they are as good as we are." As it turned out, they were indeed as good, and by the time Minasian and his cousin "Willie" Saroyan were boys early in this century, their parents' immigrant culture already constituted a major cultural presence in the Valley.

In fact, all the Valley's residents—except the Maidu, Wintun, Miwok, and Yokuts—are foreigners, and generally all have considered themselves as good as anyone else. That is why the society in this rural region remains dynamic despite constraints of economics, class, and lingering racism. Tough people from varied backgrounds, people willing to toil, have settled here and built satisfying lives—especially for their children.

As a result, those apparently empty fields shimmering east of Interstate 5 are arenas where the flawed but hopeful drama of the California Dream is performed. Buzzing south, travelers see the patches of fields, occasional houses, and hawks riding wind; they see too the dark groves where small towns dot

217

the plain. In those communities, class and ethnicity cannot be hidden or denied, and old prejudices die hard, but they are nonetheless cauldrons of change.

Kids of various colors wander barefoot over this rich soil, over these shaded streets, frequently together, with an easy multiethnicity uncomfortable to some of their elders. Those youngsters laughingly throw clods at one another, gaze silently at writhing dust devils, plunge naked into irrigation canals. And many of them, in their very assumptions about what is possible, in their determination to attend college or to marry one another or to see that this or that ethnic tradition is not allowed to disappear, challenge this state to live up to its promise, for the Valley *is* California, and so are they.

Credits

ESSAYS:

"Oil Town Rumble: The Young Men of Taft," *The Nation*, September 13, 1975. Reprinted by permission of the author.

"What about the Okies?," *American History Illustrated*, April 1997. Reprinted by permission of the author.

"William Saroyan and the Critics," *Amelia*, April 1985. Reprinted by permission of the author.

"Other Californians" ["Californians from Everywhere"], *This World*, July 7, 1987. Reprinted by permission of the author.

"Father Comes Home," *Los Angeles Times Magazine*, March 27, 1988. Reprinted by permission of the author.

"Oildale," *The Californians*, January/February 1988. Reprinted by permission of the author.

"The Other California," *Sierra*, May/June 1988. Reprinted by permission of the author.

"The Lake That Will Not Die," *Pacific Discovery*, April 1989. Reprinted by permission of the author.

"*The Grapes of Wrath*: A Book That Stretched My Soul" ["A Personal Approach to *The Grapes of Wrath*"], *California English*, May/June 1989. Reprinted by permission of the author.

"The Kern, My River" ["Taming Rio Bravo"], *Pacific Discovery*, Spring 1990. Reprinted by permission of the author.

"Remembering Hutch," *The Californians*, July/August 1990. Reprinted by permission of the author.

Western Literature Series